To Leda,

PRECISION

PATCHWORK

FOR SCRAP QUILTS

Anytime, Anywhere...

Jeannette Tousley Muir

Jeannette T. Muir

"Patchwork Forever"

PRECISION
PATCHWORK
FOR SCRAP QUILTS

Anytime, Anywhere...

Jeannette Tousley Muir

American Quilter's Society

P. O. Box 3290 • Paducah, KY 42002-3290

Muir, Jeannette Tousley
    Precision patchwork for scrap quilts : anytime, anywhere / Jeannette Tousley Muir
        p.   cm.
    Includes bibliographical references and index.
    1. Patchwork–Patterns   2. Quilting–Patterns   I. Title
TT835.M8   1995
746.46–dc20   95-9948
                                                                  CIP

Photo Credit:
All photography by Jim Muir, Moorestown, NJ; except
Plates 4-1 and 4-2 by Richard Walker, Schenevus, NY; and
Plates 4-4 and 4-10 by Gary Brown, Medford, NJ.

Additional copies of this book may be ordered from:

American Quilter's Society
P.O. Box 3290
Paducah, KY 42002-3290
@12.95. Add $2.00 for postage and handling

Printed by IMAGE GRAPHICS, INC., Paducah, Kentucky

Dedication

To Jim, for teaching me WordPerfect®,
and who, in retirement,
took over the cooking and shopping duties;
to Mom,
who instilled this love of fabrics;
and to Dad (1899–1992)
who used to say he was a quilt user.

Acknowledgments

It would take another book to name everyone who has had an influence on my life and on my work. I am definitely *not* self-taught.

Family members, teachers, students, quilters, and non-quilters, have all contributed to whatever I am, whatever I have achieved or still hope to achieve.

Specifically, I want to thank my colleagues: Pat Morris for nagging, prodding, challenging, and encouraging; Alice Mason for her travel companionship and bottomless scrap bag; and to Kay Lukasko for being a willing encyclopedia and sounding board.

Thanks to our kids, Cindy Preston, Becky MacKellar, and Doug Muir, for their assistance in giving appropriate titles to these projects.

Thanks to my fellow quiltmakers for sharing their work: Sue Ameno, Carol Boyle, Sherry Brown, Cathy Denton, Martha Eastman, Pat Gilde, Toni Hopkins, Kay Lukasko, Alice Mason, Pat Morris, Claire Regn, Teresa Thompson, and Jackie Zemaitis.

Contents

Introduction

Patchwork is a passion! I never get tired of working with fabrics – new or old, scraps or yardage. I love the whole quiltmaking process, except for the basting of the quilt sandwich. Working with fabric is immensely satisfying and therapeutic.

Time is precious, too precious to waste, and there are not enough hours in the day to make all the quilts I want to make. Perhaps because of my New England upbringing, I need to have something to do with my hands, not to be compulsive, but to be productive.

Because of this need, I worked out a very successful scheme of packaging patchwork for travel. Eight such projects have been completed over the past seven years. Although most of them were not my original designs, my need to be creative was satisfied. I made the fabric choices and the final unit placements.

Having enjoyed this entire process, and being so pleased with the results, I reasoned others would also enjoy it. I hope you will.

PATCHWORK FOREVER!!!

The Concept ====

Wouldn't you love to know how many minutes, or rather hours, of TV commercials you have watched in your lifetime? If you are a sports enthusiast like me, especially baseball, it is a considerable amount. How about during the summer and winter Olympic Games? the Open Tennis Championships? college and professional football, bowling? and so on!

There is also waiting time: at doctors' offices, airports, for the kids at music lessons and sports practices. What of the times when it is difficult to concentrate on something requiring thought? We also need "busy work" at times – just to sit and sew and be sociable, or to keep awake during marathon business meetings.

We could exercise or eat! Or we could produce something wonderful, and not thousands of paper-covered hexagons that will end up in a plastic box in the attic or at the next guild auction.

This is *not* a book about quick quilts, but about long-term projects. It specifically concerns facilitating color and fabric combinations, and packaging handwork for travel...or *anytime, anywhere.*

Chapter One — Color and Fabric

When I began quiltmaking in the mid-1970s, I thought color was baffling and befuddling, and invested many hours, as well as dollars, exploring color. I shudder to think of the untold damage done to my color thinking by my grade school teachers, especially in fourth grade. "Never, never use red and yellow together, or blue and green!" What a pity I never questioned. But back then we never questioned the teacher. She was always right.

I have read extensively. At every opportunity, I have attended seminars and workshops with nationally known personalities. I have made several color wheels; worked with transparencies, luminosity, analogous and complementary harmonies, gradations, dimension, after images, and so forth.

Finally, I comfortably reached two major conclusions. The first is to trust my own judgment; the second, the more fabrics and colors I use, the easier the design process. How's that for justifying the purchase of additional fabric! Of course, this concept is over-simplified, but it works for me. If I like it, it's right.

Color and fabric choices are always personal, but chances are, the majority of fabrics in your stash are pleasing to you, unless you have inherited someone else's inventory. Share your scrapbag, and raid that of someone else. (Alice Mason's quilts and my quilts look very similar because we love the same fabrics, most of the time.)

When someone looks at your quilt, you want them to take more than a cursory glance. You want them to notice the subtleties of fabric and color choices – pausing at one area, then moving their eyes to another location, pausing again and again. What you want to avoid is a static, boring quilt – a "walk-by."

This can be accomplished with color, contrast, and texture. But remember, if *you* like it, it's right.

YOUR PALETTE

When you spread out all your fabrics, according to value, does one color dominate? Are they entirely a warm selection – red, orange, yellow? Try adding a small portion of a cool color.

Is your palette all cool – green, blue, purple? Try adding a small portion of a warm color.

Be sure to include yellow. It can do wondrous things. Just make sure the quantity does not overpower. Chartreuse is a good substitute and is nearer to my color preference than pure yellow. The yellow fabrics currently available are spectacular. In fact, all the fabrics currently available are outstanding.

Do you have enough real *dark* darks to give your project depth? Enough *light* lights to provide contrast and highlights?

Do you have a good supply of neutrals – grays, tans, blacks, browns, whites – or as Mary Mashuta has labeled them – "pushed neutrals" – those fabrics with a hint of color in them, fabrics that are used as neutral but make the negative space much more lively and interesting?

How about an accent or a surprise? Look directly across the color wheel for that special color.

TEXTURE

Another important consideration besides color choice is the need for *variety* in the scale of design. All small prints or all the same color intensity in a quilt can be very boring and static. Using large scale prints exclusively might be too busy, but used in moderation, they provide texture and interest. Plates 1 and 2 show the results of a simple exercise in which some small-print fabrics were replaced with a few large prints. Plate 2 is much livelier and more interesting.

Plate 1.

Plate 2.

Go ahead and use your "uglies." If they really offend and stick out like sore thumbs, hide them – an interesting challenge and fun to do! You can accomplish this by lowering the contrast, making them less conspicuous.

Conversely, to promote a favorite fabric, raise the contrast, and make it more noticeable. Give it a stage.

CREATING AN INVENTORY

For beginning quilters who have absolutely *no* fabric inventory, I tell them to start collecting by coordinating their selections. They are not yet quite ready to purchase enormous quantities. (Wait until they become addicted.) I give them permission to "mess up" the quilt shop. (Most shop owners won't complain. They want to sell fabric, don't they?) Leave the kids at home. This process takes time and needs your complete concentration.

Choose one main fabric you absolutely can't live without. It can be multicolored, a larger-scale print, and should be lively and interesting. Use it as a guide for other fabric choices. Look for ten to twelve fabrics whose colors are compatible with those in the main fabric (the more the better). Each one should be mostly of the same color or a gradation of that color. These fabrics I call "tone on tone," as they do not introduce another color. The collection shown in Plate 3 may be of some help.

QUESTIONS TO ASK

Find a location in the store where you can stack these fabrics together, side by side, or one on top of another. Then, it is very important to stand back away from the stack and audition it. Ask yourself the following questions:

1. Does this combination work?
2. Does one fabric overpower/detract?
3. All warm colors? All cool?
4. Sufficient darks? Lights?
5. Is there contrast?
6. Is there a surprise?
7. Do you like it?

Dare to trust your own judgment.

Plate 3.

Chapter Two — Supplies and Terms

These items I found helpful as noted. You may find some are versatile and have other uses. Some are merely conveniences and can be done without or you can improvise as our ancestors most certainly did.

SUPPLIES

Name labels on supplies are a must if you will be with other quilters.

Batting: the quilt filling, or middle layer of the quilt sandwich

Cutting mat: a protective surface on which a rotary cutter may be used to trim seams and to cut multiple fabric layers

Even feed/walking/plaid matcher foot: a sewing machine attachment which replaces the regular presser foot and allows the three layers of the quilt sandwich to feed evenly

Fabrics: 100% cotton preferably, or your choice; the more the better!

Glue stick: to help keep a leather thimble on your finger

Graph paper: good quality, 4-to-the-inch, 8-to-the-inch, and isometric for hexagons

Iron: good quality steam iron (not a lightweight steam machine)

Ironing board: 100% cotton cover, one layer only; towel on top

Masking tape: sticky tape used to secure the backing to floor, rug, or table during the preparation of the quilt sandwich; 1½" wide works well

Needle safe: a lid-covered magnetic needle container; also houses needle threader and leather thimble; white inner surface helps needle threading visibility

Needle threader: a device to facilitate needle threading

Needles: my personal choice, #10 betweens for hand piecing; for machine quilting, Schmetz 130/705, H-Q, 11/75 or 14/90

Paper punch: ⅛" for punching holes at corners of templates

Pen: fine-point permanent red for marking templates

Pencils: for accurate marking, #2 lead mechanical, for light fabrics; Prismacolor® yellow for dark fabrics. These pencils are permanent colors. They are soft and require frequent sharpening, but mark fabric easily without distortion. The neon colors are visible on everything.

Pencil sharpener: battery operated, for home; eyebrow pencil sharpener, for away

Pin cushion: large magnetic, for home; small rolled felt, for the road

Pins: 1⅜" long, with white heads; only five or six are needed for travel

Protractor: a tool for measuring angles; may also be used for marking quilt designs

Rotary cutter: a razor-sharp cutting tool used for fast cutting and trimming seams; used with proper cutting surface underneath

Ruler: accurate see-through type, with ⅛" markings; my choice, 6" x 12" with yellow and black lines

Safety pins: 1" brass, used in basting the quilt sandwich, see Resource List

Sandpaper: gritty, fine-grade paper to slip under fabric during the marking process to prevent slippage

Scissors: your personal choice. In my traveling kit, I carry leather sheath-covered 5" craft scissors suitable for clipping and trimming. 4½" thread nippers are always by my sewing machine.

Sewing machine: optional, for quilting and binding

Stencil: pattern around which quilting designs are marked

Template: pattern for marking stitching and cutting lines on the wrong side of the fabric; see-through plastic, a good choice

Thimble: metal or leather finger protection

Thread: 100% cotton "silk finish," a good choice for both piecing and quilting; save the 100% polyester for man-made fibers

TERMS

Auditioning space: at-home area used to temporarily mount or hang the individual units, to see how they look before the final stitching

Sandwich: the quilt top, the filling, and the backing fabric

Traveling sewing kit: a container small enough to fit in your purse/large pocket, carrying only the barest of essentials

Chapter Three — The Process

This section is based specifically on the preparation sequence for MY SUNDAY BEST using the kite-shape portion of the hexagon (Jean Johnson having whetted my appetite for this shape). All succeeding projects, except those noted, were assembled using exactly the same technique. The kite is an excellent first project. The full-sized pattern included in this book was drafted to fit all those 5" charm squares that you may have collected over the years.

TEMPLATE MAKING

Some quilters are able to eyeball a perfect ¼" seam allowance. I need a visible stitching line. Accuracy is critical.

Using a fine-point permanent marking pen, transfer the corners of each pattern piece to a firm see-through plastic by marking a dot. Superimpose the ¼" line of a see-through plastic ruler on top of the dots, adding a ¼" seam allowance and solid cutting line. If desired, connect the dots with dotted lines, which represent the stitching lines. Cut on the solid line and punch out the dots with a ⅛" paper punch. Write any necessary information on the template. See sample template in Plate 4.

CUTTING

Get out all your fabrics. If you like a particular fabric, cut five or six kites. If you don't like it, cut only one. Generally the longest part of the template is placed on the straight of grain, but it is not an absolute must.

Stack cutting (introduced to me by Mary Golden) will save time. Place multiple layers of fabric together and cut all at once. Only the top fabric needs to be marked at this point. Use sharp scissors or the rotary cutter. Accuracy is not a primary concern during the cutting process. Stack cutting not only saves time, but because the sewing lines have not yet been marked, you have a future choice as to which side of the fabric to use. Frequently, the wrong side fulfills the color or shade requirement better than the right side.

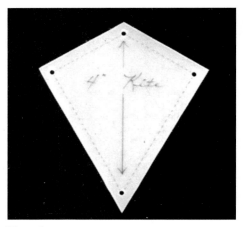

Plate 4.

15

THE SELECTION

The next sequence takes a considerable amount of time, but is the most valuable in the long run. Knowing the appearance of your finished quilt is unimportant at this point.

On a large table, spread all the kites, squares, or uncut fabrics in three rows overlapping as necessary and grading intensity from left to right, as shown in Plate 5. You can now place a value on each fabric, which is relative of course, depending on the adjacent fabric.

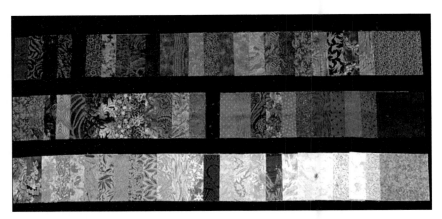

Plate 5.

To the naked eye, the color gradations in Plate 5 appear to be all wrong. Some fabrics leap out of sequence because of color or pattern. Now look at Plate 5 through a piece of red or orange Plexiglas®. You should see a distinct difference. The reds become lighter and the blues become darker.

Some fabrics, such as the cabbage rose in the center of the medium row, are always extremely difficult to place because of boldness of design. Where should it go? Is the pink fabric in the center of the light row dark or light? If some fabrics are a few settings off, no great harm is done.

(Trying to explain this technique is far more difficult than utilizing it. My own personal preference was to avoid very high contrast within each unit.)

Arbitrarily select six kites that are compatible and look attractive together – one *dark* dark, one *light* light, the other lights and darks of medium intensities.

Figure 3-1 is a placement chart suggesting possible sections of fabrics from which to select different combinations. For instance, the first unit could be composed of kites selected from Sections 1, 2, and 3; the second unit might be composed of selections from Sections 2, 3, and 4; the third, from Sections 3, 4, and 5; the next, from Sections 4, 5, and 6; then, 2, 3, and 1; and so on.

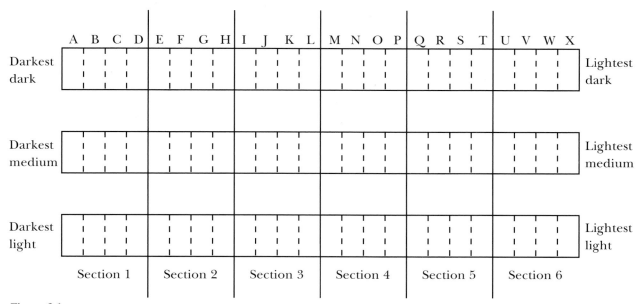

Figure 3-1.

Each six-kite unit is stacked, pinned together, and then set aside. This process may take several days, depending on the extent of your inventory, or the length of your upcoming travel, but working with fabrics is never a chore.

MARKING

Marking each piece also becomes busy work, and preferably is done at home on a flat surface with a pencil sharpener available. A piece of sandpaper placed underneath helps to control wiggly fabrics.

Placing the template on the wrong side of the fabric – or the reverse if that happens to be your choice – transfer the circles/dots to the fabric. Using one straight edge of the template, connect the dots to mark the stitching line. Be fanatical about keeping the pencil sharp, and mark lightly. The small circles/dots are much more visible at the corners, even on those difficult busy prints, than straight line intersections. The template also serves as a useful tool for "scooping up" the fabric from the sandpaper.

THE SEWING KIT

Your sewing kit should be as small as possible, carrying only the bare necessities. My kit is soft, quilted of course, measures 7½" x 4½", and can be stuffed into my purse or backpack. Its contents include: a magnetic needle safe with a lid, which houses a needle, a needle threader, and a leather thimble; a glue stick (to secure the leather thimble); 5" leather sheath-covered craft scissors; a Band Aid; an emery board; a wooden cylinder of extra needles; a 2" round, ¾" thick rolled-felt pin cushion, containing 6 pins; three shades of gray thread – light, medium, and dark; and two or three pinned-together units, depending on the duration of the flight, journey, or wait.

Plate 6.

If marking has not been done before departure, a smaller piece of sandpaper, the template, marking pencil, and small eyebrow pencil sharpener will still fit in. A hook and loop closure on the sewing kit not only keeps the flap closed, but serves as a temporary spot for disposing of loose threads.

READY FOR THE ROAD...OR WHEREVER

If you plan to travel for an extended period, put the majority of units in your suitcase and just a few in your sewing kit, replacing them as necessary. After you have stitched one unit and timed yourself, you can estimate the quantity of units required for each journey.

My friend, Kay Lukasko, asked why I hadn't told her how to determine a sufficient quantity of units for the doctor's office. She told the receptionist that the doctor should see her as soon as her handwork had been completed. How was I to know that she would have to wait three hours!

THE STITCHING

Holding any two adjoining fabric pieces, right sides together, insert a pin into corresponding circles at each end of the seam. Do not fasten the pins at this point. Find the centers of the matching lines, and insert a pin. When all three pins are exactly parallel, pinch fabrics together and fasten, taking a small bite perpendicular to the seam line (Figure 3-2). For longer seams, make sure each succeeding pin is also parallel.

(Note: Many years ago, Pat Brousil taught me the following flat-knot beginning. Pat in turn, learned it from Helen Sanders. It is simple, effective, and leaves no large lump of thread at the corner where future stitching will occur.)

Thread a needle with a 15" or less length of thread that closely matches the color of one of the fabrics. Many quilters

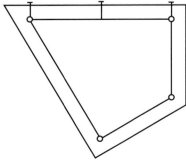

Figure 3-2.

prefer to match the darker fabric. Roll the seam inward to fit comfortably in your fist.

Insert the needle, with the unknotted thread, directly beneath the first pin, within the circle. Remove the pin, and draw up the thread, leaving a 1" tail. Flip the tail and hold it down in the seam allowance with your thumb (Figure 3-3). Take an additional stitch in the same location, but in only the left half of the circle. Draw up the thread leaving a small loop. Insert the needle up through the loop and under the tail being held by your thumb (Figure 3-4). Continue holding the tail until the next stitch is taken toward the opposite end.

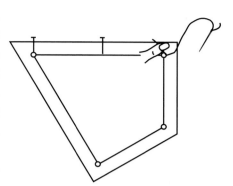

Figure 3-3.

Stitch across the remaining seam, looking occasionally to see if the lines are matching. Take a back stitch half way across. If a seam is long, especially a bias seam, back stitch about every 1½". This stitching is to last forever, so use your best, perhaps 10 to 12 stitches to the inch.

At the end of the seam, stitch only into the right half of the circle. Take an additional stitch, leaving a small loop. Insert the needle up through the loop and under the thread that is being held down with your thumb (Figure 3-5). Pull snug and clip thread, leaving a 1" tail. By stitching in only half of the circle, space is left for other seams that will eventually be stitched into the same circle.

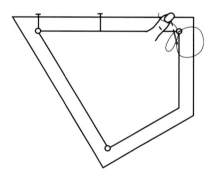

Figure 3-4.

Leave all seam allowances unstitched beyond the circles. Stitch through two layers of fabric *only* to facilitate pressing. When joining adjacent units, flip up seam allowances as you come to them, always inserting the needle directly into corresponding circles.

Trim points and excess seam allowances after the seam has been stitched. Holding the scissors palm up will help prevent accidents.

Assemble unit pieces by pairs (two pieces at a time) rather than one pair to a single piece. Use the same method for stitching rows together.

PRESSING

Pressing serves an important function in ensuring flat patchwork. Determine ahead of time in which direction seams should be pressed, and be consistent. Without a portable iron, you can finger crease the seams as you complete the stitching. As soon as possible, press each unit with a good steam iron. (Do not use a portable steam machine. Too much moisture badly distorts the fabric.)

Your ironing board should have only one 100% cotton

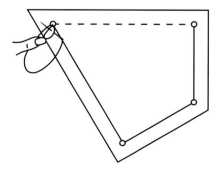

Figure 3-5.

cover. You want the steam to go through downward, rather than to bounce back at the fabric. Additionally, a towel placed under the patchwork will help keep the fabric from moving.

First, press each seam in closed position as it was stitched. Then press in the predetermined direction by scooting the iron between the layers from the right side. Allow the steam and the weight of the iron to gently work together. Do not scrub, just press quickly. You definitely will be rewarded when it is time to assemble all the units and rows. (Specific pressing directions are included with each project.)

THE AUDITION

When a sufficient number of units have been completed, put them on stage, to prepare for the final arrangement. This process should be done at home at your leisure, and not up against a deadline. Put on a tape or CD of your favorite music, relax, and prepare to stretch this audition out for many days, if necessary.

A wall is the best place to hold this audition, where you can stand back far enough to see what is going on – what it looks like – before you stitch the rows together. Attach a piece of fleece or flat batting to this wall. The fabric pieces will cling to this surface without pins. Pinning each piece to muslin or other fabric really delays the entire process. Lacking sufficient wall space, any piece of wood or cardboard covered with fleece or fuzzy flannel can serve the same purpose.

Cover the fleece haphazardly with the completed units. Do not try to place them in any particular order or location at this point.

Now, get comfortable, sit back, and look. Look through a camera lens, peephole, Plexiglas® value finder, or the wrong end of your binoculars. Squint at the wall. Leave the units there for days, if necessary. Each time you come into the room, you may get a different impression.

The first thing to look for is distractions, perhaps too many of the same fabrics or colors in the same location. Move the units to your liking. Unfortunately, each unit moved usually requires moving many others. But, to repeat myself, working with fabrics is never a chore.

At the conclusion of the audition, rows can be marked as necessary, and pinned together, ready for additional travel. At the left side of each row, in the seam allowance, draw an upward pointing small arrow. In addition, a small cloth label denoting the row number can be safety pinned. Stitched rows can easily get turned upside down wasting all your audition time.

Questions you may want to ask yourself:
- •Is it exciting? Interesting? Boring? Static?
- •Is there balance? Symmetry?
- •Is there rhythm/motion?
- •Are there highlights and shadows?
- •Does a secondary design appear?
- •Is there unity? Contrast?
- •Is there a desired repetition?

Advanced quiltmakers may be concerned with more complicated questions such as:
- •Is there a focal point?
- •Is there an overall design effect?
- •Desired asymmetry?
- •Transparency? Luminosity?
- •Texture?
- •Emotion?

The bottom line is: Do you like it?

Plate 7. *MY SUNDAY BEST, 90" x 112", Jeannette Muir, 1986 – 1992.*

Plate 8. *JUNA'S GARDEN, 47" x 57", Carol Boyle, Collingswood, NJ, 1993.*

Plate 9. *DIAMOND'S AGLO, 72" x 57", Sherry Brown, Medford, NJ, 1993*

Plate 10. *REBEC-CA'S QUILT 88" x 63", Martha Eastman, Clayton, NJ, 1993. The cathedral ceiling and large wall of her daughter's family room cried out for a quilt from Mom.*

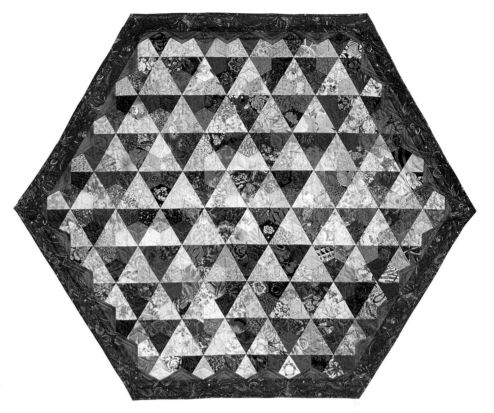

Plate 11. *PRISMS, 71" x 62", Alice Mason, Medford, NJ, 1990.*

Plate 12. *KITES, PYRAMIDS, TRIANGLES, 50" x 61", Claire Regn, Burlington, NJ, 1993. The quiltmaker's grandson saw the various shapes in this quilt, prompting the title.*

Plate 13. *SOLILOQUY, 51" x 64", Jeannette Muir.*

Plate 14. *PINWHEEL, 53" x 67", Sherry Brown, Medford, NJ, 1993. "I love scraps," says Sherry. "This one was fun and easy to make."*

25

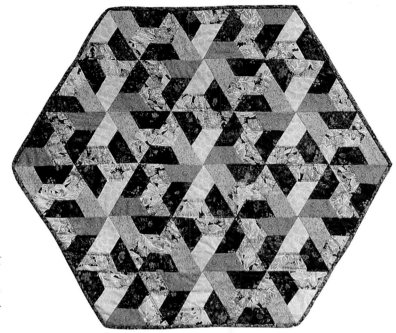

Plate 15. *NO MATTER WHICH WAY YOU LOOK AT IT, 34" x 38", Pat Gilde, Haddonfield, NJ, 1993. Made to liven up an all-white bathroom, this quilt looks like a window of mosaics, no matter which way you look at it.*

Plate 16. *SPINNING MY WHEELS, 55" x 60", Alice M. Mason, Medford, NJ, 1993.*

Plate 17. *PINWHEEL POLKA, 52" x 60", Jacqueline Zemaitis, Moorestown, NJ, 1993. This quilt has really been on the road: Pennsylvania, Virginia, Maryland, Delaware, New York, New Jersey, Massachusetts, Vermont, New Hampshire, Connecticut, Arizona, New Mexico, Utah, and Colorado.*

Plate 18. *A DARTMOUTH SEPTEMBER, 32" x 38", Toni Hopkins, Moorestown, NJ, 1993. This quilt reminded Toni of New Hampshire foliage just before the trees turn in the autumn.*

Plate 19. *YIKES! I CUT MY PLAIDS AND STRIPES, 33½" x 37", Sue Ameno, Newfield, NJ, 1993. This quilt is dedicated to Sue's grandmother, who encouraged her and her sister, Carol, to sew.*

Plate 20. *PLACEMAT, 22" x 17", Teresa Thompson, Westmont, NJ, 1993.*

Plate 21. *ALICE'S QUILT, 43" x 60", Jeannette Muir, 1991.*

Plate 22. *TRAVELING QUILT #2 – ALASKAN ODYSSEY, 68" x 60", Alice Mason, Medford, NJ, 1991. Alice pieced this quilt on a trip to Alaska, most of it on the Alaskan Highway. It is her version of the antique quilt originally seen in the storefront window in Paducah, Kentucky.*

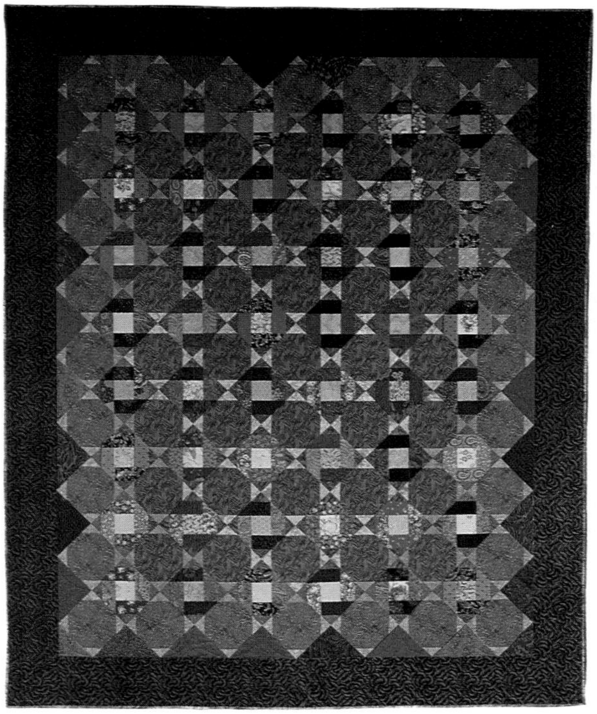

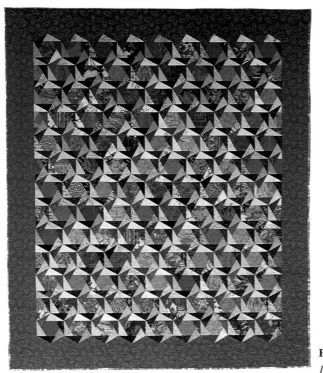

Plate 23. *CHASING GRANDMA'S DREAM, 72½ x 89½", Jeannette Muir, 1992.*

Plate 24. *PARAKEET FEET, 66" x 80", Jeannette Muir, 1993.*

Plate 25. *FEED THE BIRDS, 44" x 47", Kay Lukasko, Cinnaminson, NJ, 1993.*

Plate 26. *HOT PARADISE, 32" x 44", Patricia J. Morris, Glassboro, NJ, 1993. Naive but bold, this scrap quilt uses a limited palette of blacks, raspberry, and pinks. The asymmetrically balanced units appear to float on a black marbled print.*

Plate 27. *ERNESTINE, 74" x 84", Jeannette Muir, 1993.*

Plate 28. *SAMPRAS '93, 33" x 33", Kay Lukasko, Cinnaminson, NJ, 1993.*

Plate 29. *WILD THING, 40½" x 50", Jeannette Muir, 1993.*

Plate 30. *JEWEL ILLUSION, 29½"x 33½", Catherine M. Denton, Moorestown, NJ, 1993. A three-dimensional quality has been achieved in this variation.*

Plate 31. *CELESTIAL SEASONING, 59" x 72", Jeannette Muir, 1994.*

Chapter Four — The Projects

No yardage requirements are included because of the scrap composition of all the projects. One of the greatest charms about scrap quilts is the huge variety of fabrics used. Add to your inventory at every opportunity.

The stars next to the title of each project indicate the degree of difficulty: *Easy, **Experienced, and ***Advanced. The basic unit of each project is not complex, but joining the adjacent units can be difficult. (Project #7, KING DAVID'S CROWN, is a good example.)

Just a reminder – some templates must be traced in one direction only. This information is also included in the text.

Over the years, students have complained that one of the most difficult decisions to make is the quilting design. My own first quiltmaking experience made me painfully aware of this fact. The teacher, at the end of a ten-week course, said: "Now, take all these blocks and quilt them!" Not a word was said about sandwiching, choosing a design, or even how to quilt. Therefore, I have included a design suggestion for each project. Make quilting templates by drawing full-sized shapes onto plastic or cardboard.

Plate 32. *MY SUNDAY BEST, detail (left).*

PROJECT #1
KITES*

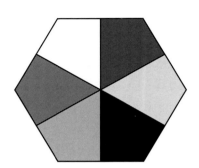

Figure 4-1.

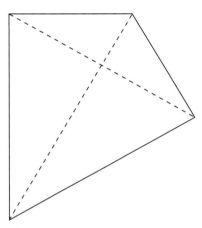

Figure 4-2.

This project uses only one shape – a kite-shaped portion of the hexagon, template A. It is called a single tessellation or mosaic-like piece. Each hexagon unit (Figure 4-1) consists of three light fabrics, each of slightly varying intensity, and three dark fabrics, also of varying intensity. Fabric placement within each unit remains consistent: the lightest light opposite the darkest dark, with medium lights and medium darks alternating as shown.

Stitch kites together in pairs, then in four, then six. Press, either clockwise, or counterclockwise but be consistent, creating a fan in the center. The seams joining adjacent units will press neatly in the opposite direction. (Refer to Chapter 3 for process.)

Ninety-seven full units and fourteen half units make up the interior portion of this project which measures 54" x 78." All fill-in segments are logically extracted from the original kite shape, as indicated by the dotted lines in Figure 4-2.

In the top and bottom rows, one angle of each unit is removed. Make sure to add a ¼" seam allowance before cutting.

Figure 4-3 shows the scale drawing with both inner and pieced borders added. Because hexagon measurements vary from top to bottom and side to side, the inner borders measure differently. The side inner borders measure 3½" in width; the top and bottom inner borders measure 3" in width. The 8" outer plain border is pictured in Plate 7, but does not appear in Figure 4-3.

Assemble the pieced border elements as large light dia-

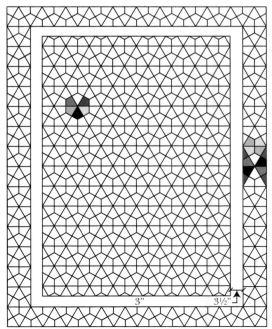

Figure 4-3.

monds and dark triangles. The side pieced borders measure 6¾" by 84"; the top and bottom borders measure 6" by 74½".

QUILTING DESIGN

The central portion of this quilt is hand quilted using a mosaic lattice design (illustrated in Figure 4-4 by the dotted lines). Only one rhomboid shape is used (Figure 4-5). Do not add seam allowances to this template. Make certain to use the template in only one position. Do not flip upside down.

Machine quilt the pieced and plain borders. I used an adaptation of a design included in the book *Continuous Line Quilting Designs* by Pat Cody.

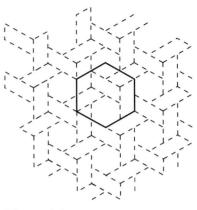

Figure 4-4.

MY SUNDAY BEST

This quilt was my first project employing my travel-packaging concept. Facing a marathon board meeting, I needed busy work to keep me awake and alert. About the same time, *The Scraplook* by Jinny Beyer was published, and I was hooked.

I cut kites from nearly every fabric in my possession. If I favored a particular fabric, I cut five or six kites. If I didn't like it, I cut only one. It challenged me to use them all.

After I had assembled 110 units, I drew the scale drawing and began the final assembly. The final assembly and the pieced border were also completed by hand.

The search for the border fabric also became a challenge, stretching out for weeks. Miraculously, one of my students had nearly a whole bolt of the perfect fabric. Her name, Sherrie Sunday, prompted the title.

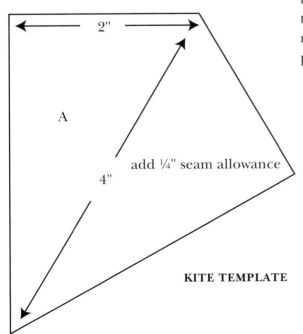

2"

A

4"

add ¼" seam allowance

KITE TEMPLATE

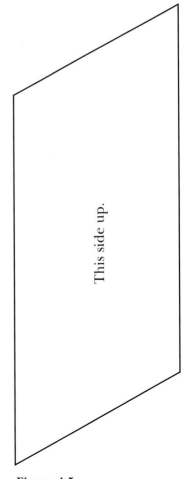

This side up.

Figure 4-5.

PROJECT #2
PINWHEEL #1*

Unit #1 (Figure 4-6) represents the first stage of putting this quilt top together, one light fabric, one medium fabric, and one dark fabric. Only one template, A, a half-hexagon, is used. The base or longest side measures 4", the other three sides measure 2".

The second stage is to select six, #1 units and assemble them into Unit #2 (Figure 4-7). The numerical piecing sequence is shown in Figure 4-8. The arrows indicate the pressing direction.

Cut the corner fill-in triangles using Template B. To make the larger side fill-in triangles, flip Template B on the dotted line marked "x."

The inner portion of SOLILOQUY, composed of 18 full #2 units, measures 39" x 52". Other portions are single #1 units.

Figure 4-6.

Figure 4-7.

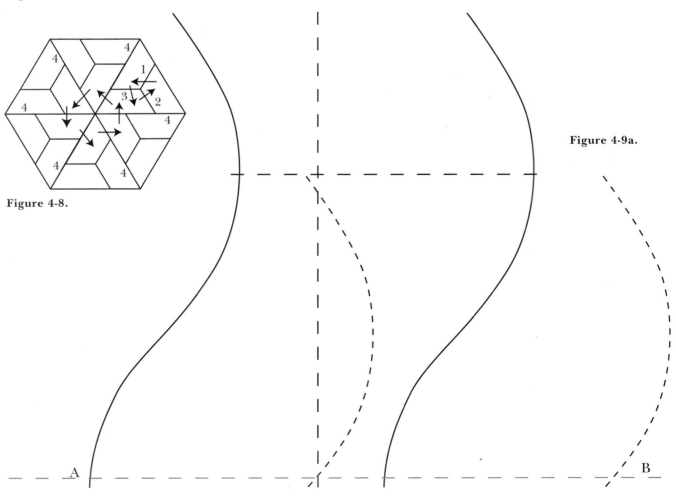

Figure 4-8.

Figure 4-9a.

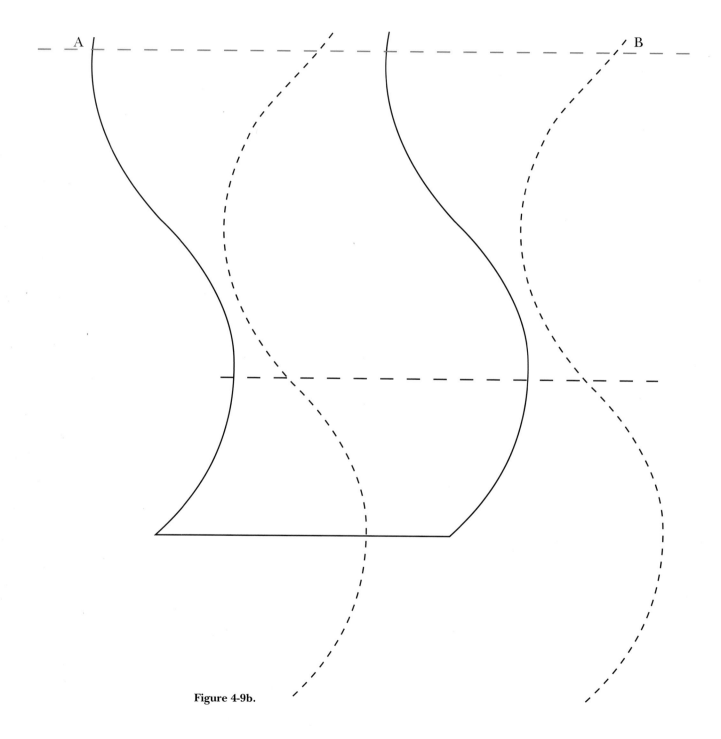

Figure 4-9b.

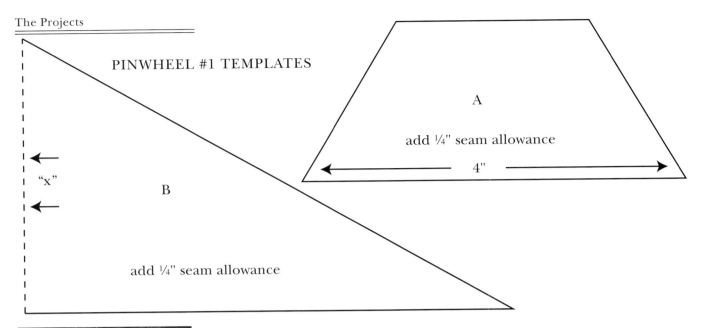

PINWHEEL #1 TEMPLATES

A

add ¼" seam allowance

4"

"x"

B

add ¼" seam allowance

Plate 33. *SOLILOQUY, detail.*

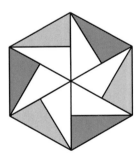

Figure 4-10.

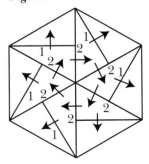

Figure 4-11.

QUILTING DESIGNS

I quilted the inner portion in thirteen parallel serpentine tracks with metallic thread as shown in Figure 4-9 a and b. Quilt additional tracks, identical to the first, between, but off-set slightly for variety. Weave ends in by hand. Quilt the borders separately. I used an adaptation of a design from Pat Cody's *Continuous Line Quilting Designs.*

Many design possibilities occur using just this one shape. It can easily be re-drafted to meet your size requirements.

This quilt is more like a color wash with very low contrast using the fabrics that I love. It was so named because of the conversations I had with myself during the audition process. (It is in the collection of Cynthia Muir Preston.)

PROJECT #3
PINWHEEL #2*

The two quilts shown in Plates 18 and 19 are excellent examples of the wide variety possible using exactly the same shape, a single tessellation.

Twelve pieces make up each hexagon unit as shown in Figure 4-10. The interior stars are light in this case, but can be dark, medium, or randomly placed.

Prepare template A, adding the construction circle marked "a." When marking fabric, be sure to flip (reverse) the template, as necessary. Example: if you choose the fabric placement as shown in Figure 4-10, cut all the lights in one

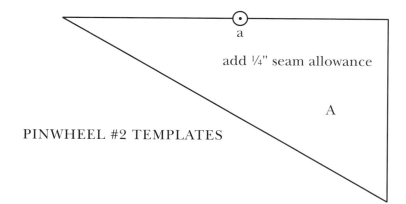

PINWHEEL #2 TEMPLATES

add ¼" seam allowance

a

A

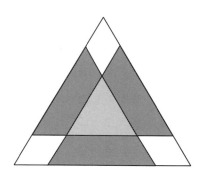

Figure 4-12.

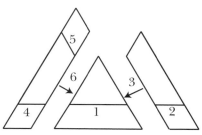

Figure 4-13.

from wrong side

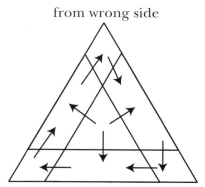

Figure 4-14.

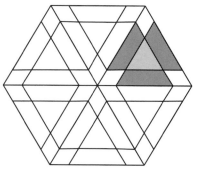

Figure 4-15.

direction, flipping the template for all other fabrics.

Matching pairs at "a," stitch into equilateral triangles. Continue numerical piecing sequence as shown in Figure 4-11. Arrows indicate suggested pressing direction.

A DARTMOUTH SEPTEMBER, a random placement in shades of green, contains a surprise splash of red/orange to add sparkle. It is quilted in the ditch in large diamond grids.

YIKES! I CUT MY PLAIDS AND STRIPES represents a more traditional placement of fabric and color, each piece being carefully cut using identical grain placement. Sue used a smaller template for this piece, the longest side measuring 3" instead of 4". She quilted it in the ditch in diagonal lines 1¼" apart. Alternate lines stop at the inner edge of the red border.

PROJECT #4

NEW HAMPSHIRE (VARIATION) **

Two separate stages make up the preparation for this project. The first is to assemble the units shown in Figure 4-12. Each unit consists of three diamonds, template A, in varying intensities of light fabrics; one equilateral triangle, template B, in medium fabrics; and three trapezoids, template C, of the same dark fabric. (Option: three different darks.)

Figure 4-13 indicates the numerical piecing sequence.

Looking at the wrong side of the stitched unit, press in the directions indicated by the arrows in Figure 4-14. Be consistent. Adjoining unit segments will fan in the opposite direction.

In the second stage, select six of the prepared #1 units (Figure 4-12) to pin together for further travel and to stitch into full hexagons as shown in Figure 4-15. (I tried to make sure each of the six diamonds that formed the center star were of different light fabrics.) Star points will press easily in a fan formation.

39

Make a template from the drawing labeled "D" for the corner fill-in triangles. Be sure to reverse or flip the template as necessary.

For the long-side fill-in triangles, flip the template on the dotted line marked "x," or make a separate template. For the top and bottom fill-in triangles, flip the template on the dotted line marked "y."

QUILTING DESIGN

Figure 4-16 indicates a portion of the suggested/optional quilting track specifically designed to highlight the light stars. Each row extends to the outer edge and requires no beginnings or endings within the body of the quilt. Horizontal tracks are shown; diagonal tracks are shown in blue and black. Quilt the

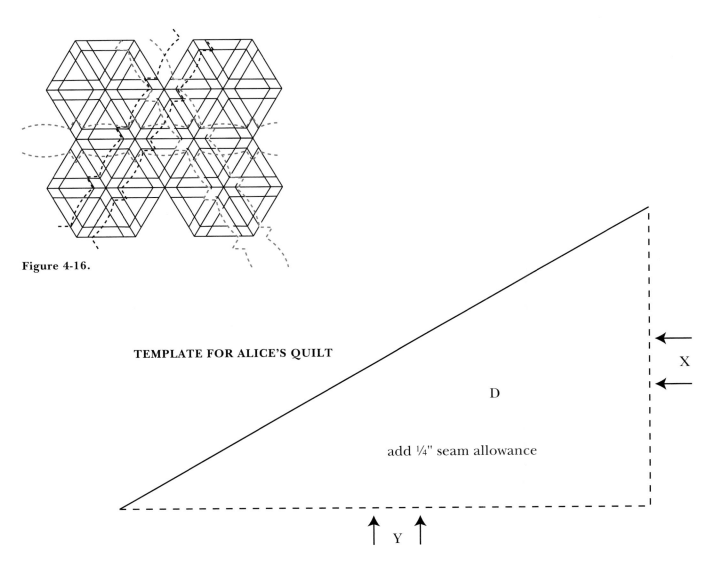

Figure 4-16.

TEMPLATE FOR ALICE'S QUILT

D

add ¼" seam allowance

X

Y

lines immediately adjacent to the star points in the ditch. A simple circle with a radius of 3½" was used for the curve.

ALICE'S QUILT

The pattern source books call this basic design New Hampshire, or Florida, among many other titles. I was introduced to it in an antique quilt display in a Paducah, Kentucky, storefront window. None of the examples showed the center star points with light fabrics. Remembering that light advances, I knew such a coloration would be successful.

In an effort to stay awake and alert during the long drive to Paducah, Kentucky, to attend the AQS Annual Show, we read "Trivial Pursuit®" questions to each other. Alice disagreed with my answer of "Australia." "Are you sure?" she said. "Would you bet your quilt on it?" The warmest continent is Africa, of course! I gave her a photo of the quilt and named it after her. Isn't that sufficient!

Other possible variations are shown in Figures 4-17a and 4-17b, and in *Key to a Second 1000 Quilt Patterns* by Judy Rehmel, designs #1513 and #1514.

A wider border might have been more suitable, but would not have fit the wall space reserved for this quilt.

Plate 33a. *ALICE's QUILT, detail. ALICE's QUILT consists of fifteen #2 units (Figure. 4-15). Sixteen #1 units (Figure 4-12) fill in the remaining spaces. The total number of #1 units is 106.*

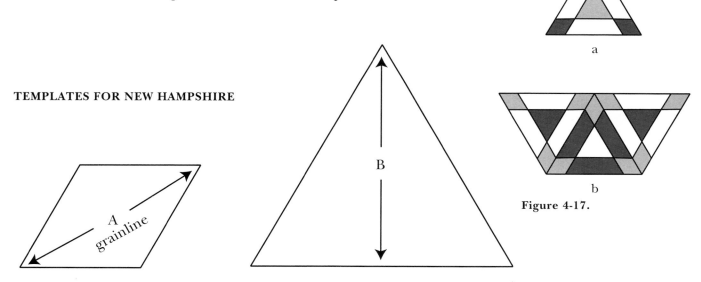

a

b

Figure 4-17.

TEMPLATES FOR NEW HAMPSHIRE

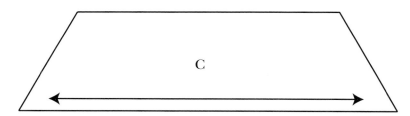

A grainline

B

add ¼" seam allowances

C

41

Plate 34. *CHASING GRAND-MA'S DREAM, detail. The setting for CHASING GRANDMA'S DREAM was found in* The Pieced Quilt *by Jonathan Holstein. The logo of a major banking institution inspired the original unit, Figure 4-18.*

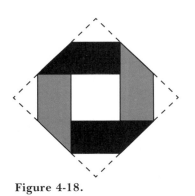

Figure 4-18.

Figure 4-19.

PROJECT #5
OCTAGON TILE**

The quilt itself is made up of 48 Octagon Tile blocks, alternately set with 63 Melon Patch blocks. Draft it as you would draft a kaleidoscope and not as a Nine-Patch Snowball.

For the initial unit as shown in Figure 4-18, two templates are required: A, a 2½" square, and B, a trapezoid measuring 2½" on one side and 4¼" on the parallel side. Cut the square from light fabrics, the sides from medium and dark fabrics. Punch an extra hole, indicated by circle "a," on template B. It is very helpful during construction.

Use template B in one direction only, either face up or face down. When cutting and marking fabrics, make sure not to flip it. If you stack your fabric for faster cutting, all pieces should be either face up or face down, and should not be folded.

As shown in Figures 4-19 and 4-20, the piecing sequence is a bit different from the other projects. Beginning with any A and B pair, with right sides together, stitch part way (about 1¼") across the initial seam. Back stitch and leave thread uncut as shown to be picked up later for seam #5.

Proceed in numerical sequence as detailed in Figure 4-20. Seam #5 is the completion of the initial seam. Arrows in Figure 4-20 indicate the direction in which to press the seams.

Because the octagon does not tessellate (fit like a mosaic) as the hexagon does, use an extra template C to make the octagons into squares. These may be added during the initial unit construction, or later when final placement decisions have been made.

Also use Template C as the "ears" with template D to create the alternate block, the Melon Patch (Figure 4-21).

For an on point or diagonal set, use template E for all fill-in spaces, except the corners which are cut from template F. In CHASING GRANDMA'S DREAM, a variety of fabrics was used for corners and for fill-in spaces.

QUILTING DESIGN

An optional quilting design is shown in Figure 4-22. Four separate tracks run diagonally through each Octagon Tile block, partly in the ditch, as shown by the red, green, blue, and black dashes.

Additionally, four separate tracks shown in red, green, blue, and black dots and dashes run diagonally through the Melon Patch blocks.

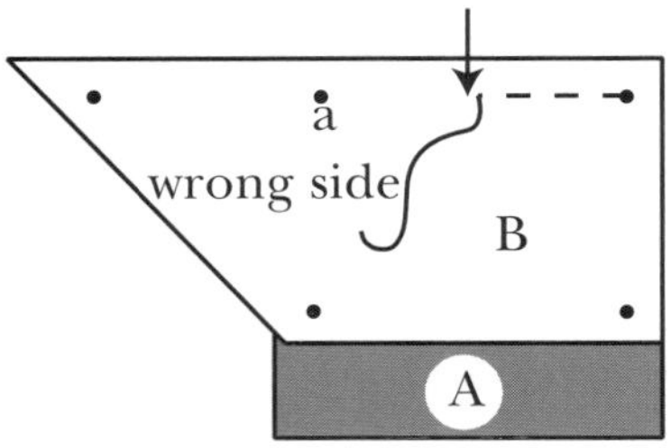

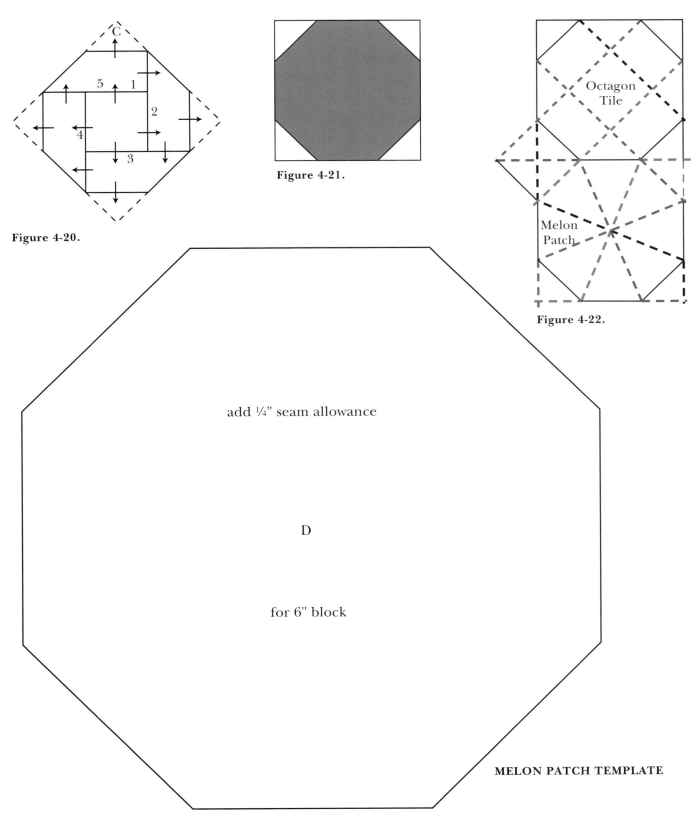

Figure 4-20.

Figure 4-21.

Octagon Tile

Melon Patch

Figure 4-22.

add ¼" seam allowance

D

for 6" block

MELON PATCH TEMPLATE

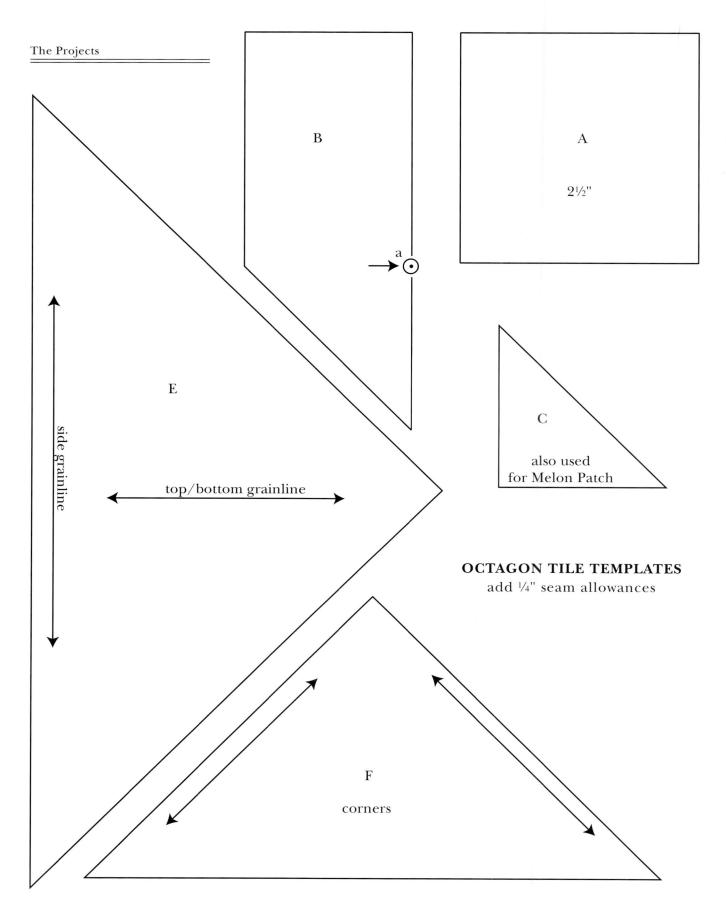

B

A

2½"

a

E

side grainline

top/bottom grainline

C

also used
for Melon Patch

OCTAGON TILE TEMPLATES
add ¼" seam allowances

F

corners

PROJECT #6
HUB CAP**

The basic unit is shown in Figure 4-23. Cut all center hexagons, template A, from medium fabrics; cut scalene triangles, template B, from light and dark fabrics. Be sure to transfer construction circle, "a."

Trace template B in one position only. Do not flip template. It will work in either direction, but be consistent. Write a message to yourself directly on the template. (My personal message reads, "This side up on wrong side of fabric.") If stack cutting, make certain that all fabrics face the same direction.

Beginning with any A and B combination, pin right sides together as shown in Figure 4-24. Stitch half way across the seam, about 1" only; take a small backstitch, and leave the thread uncut. Gently finger crease the seam toward the triangle. Resume numerical piecing sequence as shown in Figure 4-25. The arrows indicate the pressing direction. Be consistent. It is very important to thoroughly press and trim the seams of each unit before it is joined to an adjacent unit. Notice that the seams joining the hexagons are pressed in alternate directions – the lights toward the center, and the darks toward the outside. This may seem unusual at this point, but will greatly ease the joining and pressing of the adjacent units. Six-point junctures will conveniently fan in opposite directions.

Make template C for the top and bottom fill-in triangles. The corner fill-in triangles are half of C as indicated by the dotted line.

QUILTING DESIGN

For the optional quilting design, run six separate tracks through each unit. The first three, represented in Figure 4-26 by red, green, and blue dots and dashes, were marked using an 8" protractor. The next three tracks, represented by red, green, and blue dashes (Figure 4-27), were marked with an arc with a radius of 7½".

PARAKEET FEET

The design for PARAKEET FEET came directly from an automobile hub cap. Although a pentagon, it was easily drafted into a hexagon (Figure 4-23). When the scale drawing, Figure 4-28 was completed, for some reason it made me think of bird tracks. The title PARAKEET FEET stuck with this quilt.

The quilt itself is composed of 111 full units (Figure 4-23) and 12 half-units. These half-units were actually 12 full units cut in half, adding ¼" seam allowance at the cut.

Plate 35. *PARAKEET FEET, detail.*

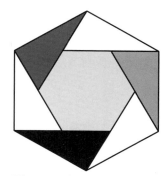

Figure 4-23.

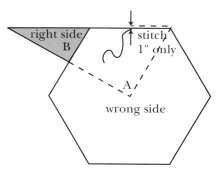

Figure 4-24.

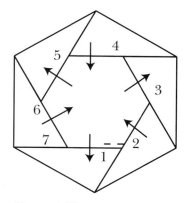

Figure 4-25.

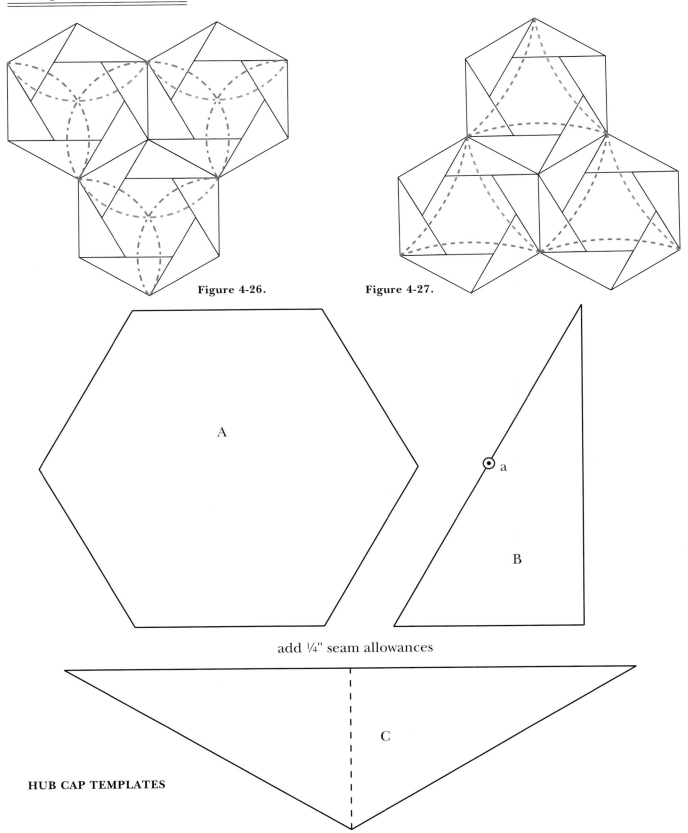

Figure 4-26.   Figure 4-27.

A

B

⊙ a

add ¼" seam allowances

C

HUB CAP TEMPLATES

Although very subtle, the bright pink fabric placement was deliberate to form two diagonal lines. This started to happen accidentally during the audition process, and with a little extra arranging, was completed.

Alternating rows of high contrast would undoubtedly be very effective and dramatic, perhaps one of my next projects.

PROJECT #7
KING DAVID'S CROWN***

This project is designated *** because of the final assembly or the setting of the units. The initial units themselves, are easily drafted on a 25-square grid and are wonderfully simple to assemble. Figure 4-29 shows the only two templates, A and B, needed for the unit. Be sure to transfer the construction circle marked "a." Figure 4-30 represents the numerical piecing sequence. The arrows indicate suggested pressing direction.

Use template C for the setting pieces that join the blocks together. Cut vertical pieces with the longest portion on the straight of grain, horizontal pieces with the shortest width on the straight of grain. Match seams at circles "a."

The long half of template C is used for all fill-in pieces.

Figure 4-31 illustrates the procedure for stitching the rows together.

QUILTING DESIGN

All quilting tracks begin and end at the outside edge, requiring no weaving of ends or securing of stitches, except those that will not be covered with the binding. For better visibility, Figures 4-32 and 4-33 illustrate two differ-

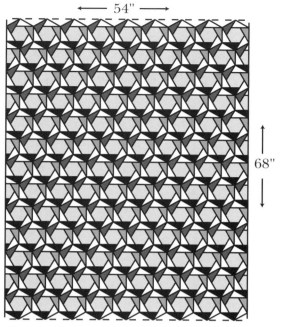

Figure 4-28.

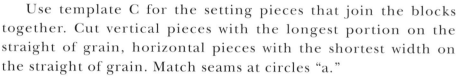

Figure 4-29.

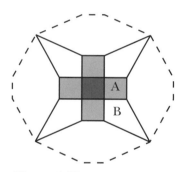

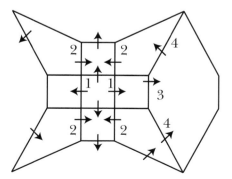

Figure 4-30.

Figure 4-31.

47

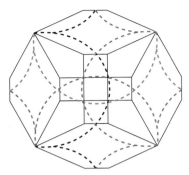

Figure 4-32.

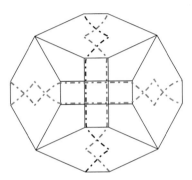

Figure 4-33.

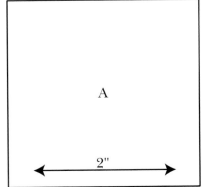

Plate 36. *ERNESTINE, detail.*

ent quilting designs. Blue and black dashes indicate the vertical tracks. Red and green represent the horizontal tracks.

Additional unmarked tracks are quilted in the ditch adjacent to each block in all directions.

ERNESTINE

Considering I did not choose the fabrics, except for the background, this quilt represents quite a departure from the original concept.

When I first saw this top, "Improved (!) Nine-Patch," of the 1940s at the vendor's booth, Vintage Tools and Textiles, it was the ugliest thing I had ever seen! All the squares were red, the background was muslin (the quality of cheesecloth), but the other fabrics were great. The construction was unbelievable. Thread was wrapped around the intersection, and the needle inserted through the wrapping. I immediately fell in love with it, and the price was right. It made me, and everyone else, laugh!

Picking apart the blocks, replacing the center squares and a few other parts with 1940s fabrics, became busy work. Each of the 56 blocks was recut, remarked, and pinned together, for another long-term project. I am not laughing anymore, but I sure am smiling! Thanks Helen, Julie, and Kathy.

add ¼" seam allowances

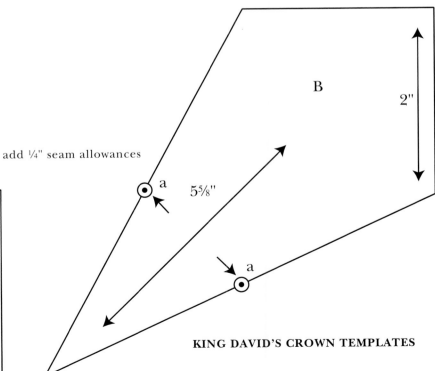

KING DAVID'S CROWN TEMPLATES

A

2"

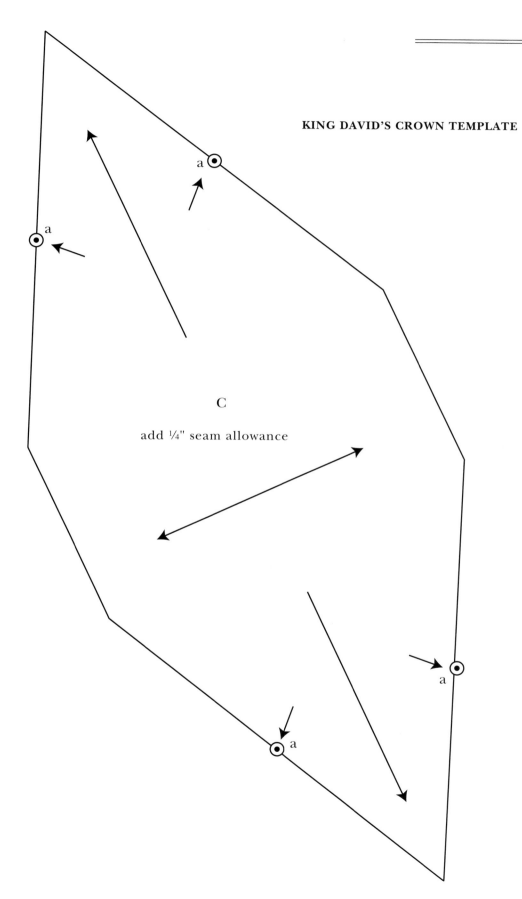

KING DAVID'S CROWN TEMPLATE

C

add ¼" seam allowance

Plate 37. *WILD THING, detail.*

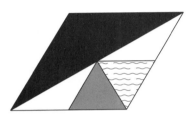

Figure 4-34.

PROJECT #8
HEXAGON JEWEL***

Although the basic unit is not difficult to assemble, joining the twelve-points of adjacent units is definitely not easy, hence the degree of difficulty assigned this project.

WILD THING appears to be made of triangles, but in fact, it is hexagons. Figure 4-34 shows the first travel unit. Use templates A, B, and C. Be sure to transfer the construction circle labeled "a."

Piece in the numerical sequence indicated in the upper left section of Figure 4-35. Press seams in the direction shown.

Notice that one seam in each #1 unit is pressed open to circle "a." Although this seems unusual, it facilitates the final assembly and pressing of the 12-point junctures.

Select three #1 units to create the full hexagon (Figure 4-35) to make up the second travel package.

To achieve a three-dimensional appearance when the units are stitched together, try to maintain a consistent placement of the dark fabrics. In Figure 4-36, "dd" indicates placement for the darkest dark; "md" the medium dark; and "ld" the lightest dark.

Figure 4-35.

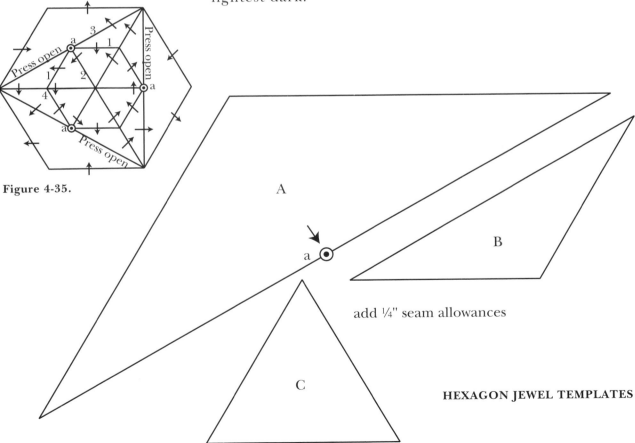

add ¼" seam allowances

HEXAGON JEWEL TEMPLATES

Thirty-two full #2 units, (Figure 4-35) make up this top. Side fill-ins are half of unit 1. Cut top and bottom fill-ins from template A; corners are half of template A. Flip as necessary.

QUILTING DESIGN

Figure 4-37 shows an optional quilting design. Run three separate tracks of straight lines through each unit. These are indicated by red, green, and blue dots and dashes and are stitched with a lighter thread.

Three separate tracks of curved lines also run through each unit. These are indicated by red, green, and blue dashes and are stitched with a darker thread.

WILD THING

WILD THING is named in tribute to the wonderful baseball summer of 1993, as provided by the Philadelphia Phillies and notorious relief (!) pitcher, "Wild Thing" Mitch Williams.

The design was doodled a number of years ago while attending a Helen Thompson workshop entitled "Jeweled Cube."

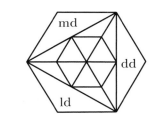

Figure 4-36.

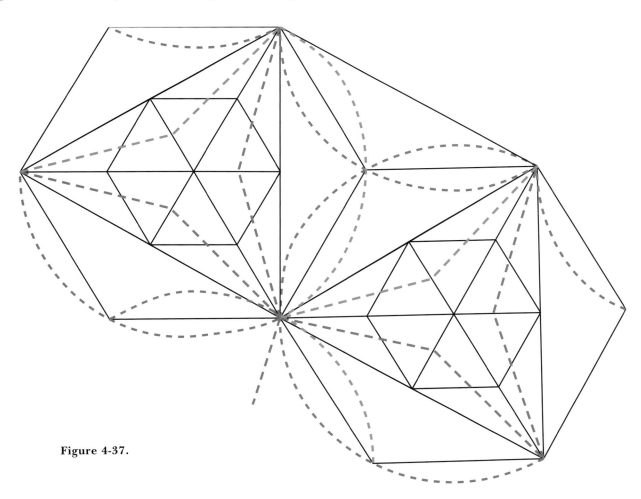

Figure 4-37.

Plate 38. *CELESTIAL SEASON-ING, detail.*

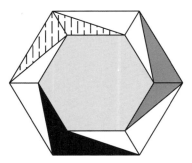

Figure 4-38.

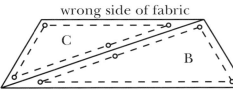

Figure 4-39.

PROJECT #9
BOOMERANG***

Use three templates to complete each unit (Figure 4-38), one hexagon, A, and two slightly different scalene triangles, B and C. Be sure to mark circle labeled "a" for construction purposes. Three light and three dark "boomerangs," all of varying intensity, make up each unit. Cut the hexagons from medium fabrics.

To avoid losing small pieces, trace B and C on the same piece of fabric (Figure 4-39). Cut apart when ready to stitch. Making a sample block/unit before marking and cutting all the fabrics is a good idea. Because it is easy to mark these pieces upside down (the wrong way around), I write a reminder to myself on each template, "This side up on wrong side of fabric." A little planning ahead ensures that the correct combinations will be stitched together. As usual, place the lightest fabric combination opposite the darkest combination.

Begin the stitching sequence by selecting any B and C combination, one light and one dark. With right sides together, match reference circles "a" and stitch seam as shown in Figure 4-40. Finger press toward the darker fabric. Continue stitching all matching pairs together, or stitch each pair to the hexagon "A" as soon as completed. Stitch the short 1½" seams last using matching thread.

Figure 4-41 shows the suggested numerical piecing sequence with the arrows indicating the direction in which to press the seams. Although the pressing instructions seem unusual at this time, they simplify the final assembly. Finger crease after each seam is stitched. Steam press and trim the seams before stitching adjacent units together. Intersections will fan and press flat.

Template D is used for the side fill-in triangles. The corners are half of D, as indicated by the dotted line.

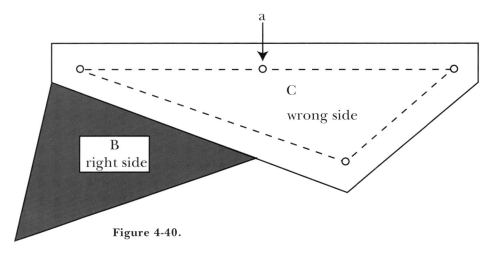

Figure 4-40.

QUILTING DESIGN

Figures 4-42, and 4-43 detail optional quilting designs. Stitch all straight lines in the ditch.

Six separate tracks run through each unit and may be extended through the border to the outside edge, or quilt the border separately. Each track is shown in a different color of dashes in Figure 4-42 and dots and dashes in Figure 4-43.

CELESTIAL SEASONING

CELESTIAL SEASONING consists of 53 complete #1 units and six half units. Be sure to add ¼" seam allowances to the half portion being used. A narrow ¾" inner border was added to create a floating appearance.

A more limited fabric selection was used for this quilt – approximately 12 lights and 12 darks. Actually, only one multi-shaded medium fabric was used for the hexagons, but it was separated into about twelve different stacks.

The design for this quilt was seen during the summer of 1993 on a broadcast of *Good Morning America* from the Great Barrier Reef, Australia. The design appeared on a T-shirt worn by a boomerang demonstrator.

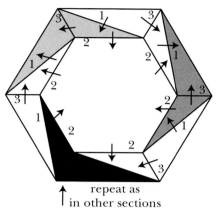

Figure 4-41.

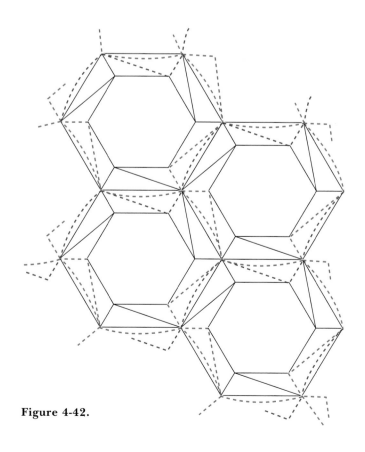

Figure 4-42.

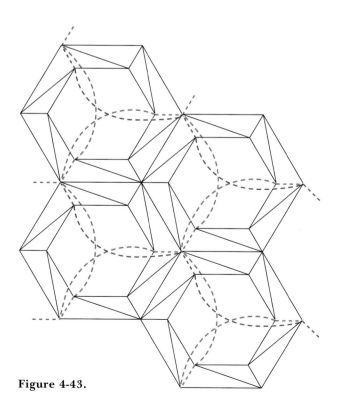

Figure 4-43.

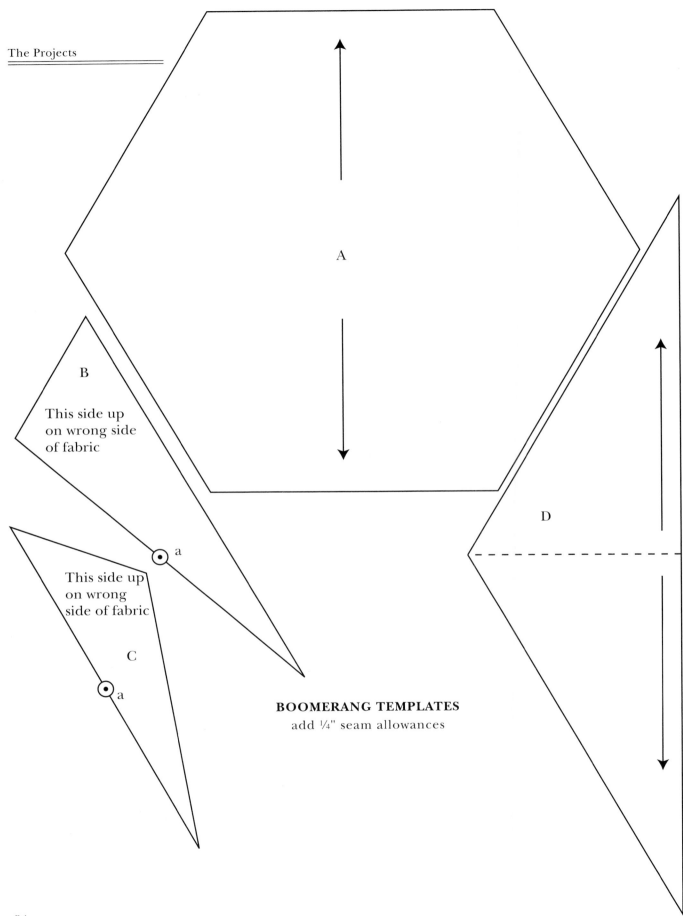

A

B

This side up
on wrong side
of fabric

⊙ a

This side up
on wrong
side of fabric

C

⊙ a

D

BOOMERANG TEMPLATES
add ¼" seam allowances

Chapter Five — Borders

COLOR

FABRIC

OTHER CONSIDERATIONS

WIDTH

MITERED OR BUTTED

MEASURING

APPLYING THE BORDER

Rarely do I know ahead of time what my quilt borders will be, either in color, fabric, or size. I usually return to the audition wall for this information.

The first question is, "Does it need a border?" Borders are not always necessary. Many of the antique quilts we love so much do not have a border. However, in my opinion, perhaps because of the sheer number of fabrics used in scrap quilts, a border looks better. It provides a frame to keep the fabrics under control. Is this piece for a bed or for the wall? All sides do not necessarily need a border. You make the choice, and anything goes!

Perhaps out of a sense of economy, I begin with fabrics already in my inventory. I pin the top to the wall and drape folded segments of fabrics at the side. However, I usually make another trip to the quilt shop. (Not a hardship!)

This trip presents another opportunity for you to mess up the store. Be sure to take the top with you and leave the kids at home. It is an exciting time, so don't hurry this process. If you have a patient friend whose judgment you trust, take him/her along for affirmation. However, reserve the right to make the final decision yourself.

COLOR

Usually you already have an idea about which color you intend to use, but not always. PARAKEET FEET is a case in point. I was almost certain my color choice would be dark teal or dark blue.

Tuck a portion of your top into one of the store shelves and unfold enough bolts of fabric along side to really see what happens. Then walk to the other end of the shop. Ask yourself:
•Are these fabrics compatible?
•Does one fabric enhance or detract?
•Does this fabric overpower or disappear?
•Does it do anything?
•Does it highlight your accent color?

FABRIC

When you have settled on a color, look next at the print/design of the fabric itself. Are the figures too large or regularly patterned that they immediately call attention to themselves, totally dominating the quilt top? Or is there a perfect blend that adds interest and texture to the overall appearance?

Trust your judgment!

OTHER CONSIDERATIONS

Does the quilt need an additional inner border? Perhaps the perfect outer border fabric is a bit too strong and needs an intermediate fabric to cushion the shock. Should this inner border be lighter or darker in color? Perhaps multiple borders, narrow to wide, would work well.

Frequently borders consist of large pieces of several fabrics and sizes which would be appropriate for a scrap quilt. However, if you decide on a fancy pieced border, a worksheet is probably helpful. Look for help in one of the many excellent books on the subject, *Blocks and Borders* by Jinny Beyer, *Quilt Settings* by Marie Shirer, and *Sets & Borders* by Marston and Cunningham.

You have other options. For instance, a single fabric border is usually a good choice for a scrap quilt. If applique is your strong point, by all means use it. There are many other choices. Check your favorite books and magazines for the border that works best for you.

WIDTH

The width of a border or borders is your personal choice. However, adding too many borders in the attempt to make a small quilt large, leads to the border becoming the dominant feature of the quilt. If you choose a wide border, quilt it in a quantity consistent with the center portion quilting. Remember, if you plan to quilt fancy feather designs, a busy print hides all your efforts.

MITERED OR BUTTED?

Most of the projects in this book have borders that are butted together at the corners rather than mitered, mainly because there are no right angles in a hexagon. However, a regularly patterned fabric is usually more attractive with mitered corners.

Side borders are usually added before the top and bottom borders, but this sequence can be reversed if the fabric quantity dictates.

If the quilt is to hang, it is a good idea to cut the long sides on the straight of the grain. My choice is to cut the side borders on the lengthwise grain and the top and bottom borders across grain.

MEASURING

Whichever border color, design, or width you choose, you must measure accurately, not at the edges, but straight down the center for the side borders and straight across the center for the top and bottom borders. A quilt with unintentionally ruffled sides probably had too much border fabric applied.

Many quilters advise not tearing fabrics. I tear only with the straight of grain. I have already determined if a fabric will not tear well when I removed the selvedges. Tear or cut the fabric several inches longer than the preliminary measurement indicates.

Large quilts frequently require piecing fabrics to make the borders long enough, especially across the top and bottom. Miter two pieces as shown in Figure 5-1. Trim the seam allowance to ¼" and press open (Figure 5-2).

APPLYING THE BORDER

Press the top and place it wrong side up on a flat surface. Measure down the center of the quilt, seam line to seam line. If you need a stitching line as I do, draw the required measurements directly on the wrong side of the border fabric. Be sure to add ¼" seam allowances. Cut identical side borders.

To make the top fit the border, place a pin in the exact center of the top's side and another in the center of the border. Place together the right sides of the border and top. Then with the wrong side of the pieced top toward you, match center pins and fasten. Match the corners and pin. Find the mid-point between pins and pin again. Continue in this manner, easing the fabric evenly as necessary. Stitch.

Repeat for the opposite side. Carefully press seams away from the center. Again, place the top on a flat surface and measure across the center and the added side borders to determine the measurement of the top and bottom borders. Cut and mark identical top and bottom borders.

Mark quilt top and border centers with pins as before and stitch together. Press the seams toward the borders.

Press the entire top. Hang it temporarily on the wall and admire it for a few days before beginning the tedious chore of preparing the sandwich.

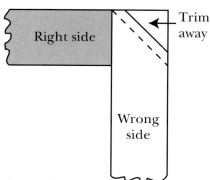

Figure 5-1.

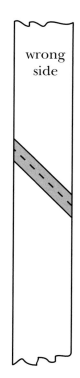

Figure 5-2.

Chapter Six — Quilting

Undoubtedly, some quilters would consider machine quilting a hand pieced top heresy! I certainly gave it a great deal of thought before coming to the conclusion that I simply would never finish the quilting otherwise. There are so many quilts I want to make. And where is it written that a handmade top cannot be machine quilted? (If you are a confirmed hand quilter, excellent books on the subject are available, especially, *The Ins and Outs: Perfecting the Quilting Stitch* by Patricia J. Morris.)

Machine quilting is finally getting some recognition and respect. Many major shows now offer separate prizes for both hand and machine quilted entries. Machine quilted does not mean the quilts are inferior. They can be every bit as admired as those quilted by hand. Workmanship does not have to be compromised.

HAND VS. MACHINE

Exactly what is quilting and what is its purpose? It is small running stitches, consistent in length, which hold the sandwich together – the top, the batting/filler, and the backing. Quilting also adds dimension, enhances the design of the top, and discourages wrinkling. The stitches and subsequent design on a solid color fabric become more visible, while on a busy print the stitches hide, and fancy designs are lost.

Up to this point, the same criteria applies for both hand and machine quilting. But there are some real differences. Hand quilting is much softer in appearance. Only one strand of thread is used and there are spaces between the stitches. Machine quilting appears harsh. Two threads are used, the top thread and one in the bobbin with no spaces between the stitches.

Hand quilting is slow, requiring great patience. It is restful, unless you are up against a deadline. Machine quilting is quick, but also requires patience. It can sometimes be exhausting.

Hand quilting, except when done on a large frame, is portable and can be social; machine quilting is neither of these. But, the one great advantage to using the machine, besides time, is the ability to quilt through multiple seam allowances with ease. It is not a design deterrent.

METHODS

Basically, two methods are used for machine quilting. One uses a machine attachment called a walking foot. The other, free motion quilting, is done by lowering the feed dogs of the machine. My expertise lies entirely with the first-mentioned method. For information on free motion quilting, see the bibliograpy which lists several excellent books on this subject.

EQUIPMENT

Obviously, first you need a decent sewing machine. It does not have to be the fanciest top-of-the-line model, but a good one is worth its weight in gold and causes far fewer headaches. Like many other things, buy the best you can afford.

Consult with your friends and relatives. Word of mouth endorsements mean a lot. A reputable dealer is an absolute must. Don't be afraid to take fabric with you, or in this case a prepared fabric sandwich. You have the right and privilege as a consumer to check out what you purchase, especially such an important and expensive item.

Look for ease of operation, a consistent stitch, a large-size bobbin, dependability, and a light (or lights) placed directly above the needle. (The presser foot lifter of the Bernina is indispensable.) If you use the machine a great deal, plan to take it in for a yearly physical, keep it clean, oil only as necessary, sing to it, and make it a machine quilted cover. In *The Creative Machine,* Robbie Fanning exhorts us to "Hug Your Sewing Machine."

A special luxury item is a table with a well, so the throat plate is level with the table. A corner table is a good choice. With walls on two sides, the quilt can be piled up to the ceiling and will never drop off. And, you can rest your elbows.

Next you need a walking/even-feed foot, sometimes called a plaid matcher. It is a wonderful box-like contraption that replaces the regular all-purpose foot allowing the sandwich to feed evenly. For hand quilters, it is well worth buying if only to apply the binding. See your sewing machine dealer or the Resource List for a machine mail-order catalog. Before ordering, you need to know the machine brand name and model number, if it has a straight or slant needle or long or short shank.

Start each project with a new needle, size 11/75 or 14/90 (see supply list) depending on the fabric and thread used.

Expect to change needles frequently as the polyester content in the batting dulls them. A bent needle or one with a burr, can seriously damage the bobbin case, cause skipped stitches, or mar your fabric.

BATTING

Batting is a very personal choice, each quilter having a favorite selection. I personally prefer Cotton Classic® by Fairfield mainly because of the ease in handling, the way it prevents fabrics from slipping, its low loft, and my preference for a flat quilt. It contains 80% cotton and 20% polyester. Fleece also works well, but perhaps is too stiff for a crib quilt or garment.

Avoid using any ultra or extra loft batting. The walking foot tends to hang up on bulky seam allowances thereby causing the machine to stitch in place, rather than to feed evenly.

BACKING

The backing fabric should be as busy as possible so any stitch length irregularity will be less visible, particularly if you have changed thread color frequently or have many beginnings and endings to hide. Make sure the backing fabric is of good quality and compatible in color and fiber content with the top. Loosely woven fabric will not support the stitches and quilting detail will be lost. Purchase an additional ½ yard to reserve for the display sleeve.

If the backing needs to be pieced, use ⅜" to ½" seam allowances and press open. I prefer two vertical symmetrically placed seams, rather than one down the center, especially if it is a wall hanging. This helps prevent the distracting crease in the center if the quilt has been folded in half instead of in thirds.

PREPARATION OF THE SANDWICH

Proper preparation of the sandwich, my least favorite part of the entire quiltmaking process, is absolutely critical for successful machine quilting. It cannot be stressed enough. Invite your friends for lunch and be prepared to reciprocate, perhaps offering to apply a binding.

Thoroughly tape the well-pressed backing (approximately 4" larger than the top), right side down on the floor, low-pile rug, or protected table if the piece is small, smoothing out all wrinkles. It should be taut, but not stretched. Smooth the batting over the backing. (Do not tape the batting.) Cover the batting with the well-pressed top, matching center sides and center top and bottom.

Beginning in the middle and working toward the lower edge, insert 1" brass safety pins (see Resource List) 2½" to 3" apart. Do not fasten at this time. Repeat pinning from middle to top and middle to sides. Continue pinning in grid fashion, filling all spaces. Pin around the entire perimeter, ¼" to ½" from the raw edge at much closer intervals. Straight pins can be used for the outside edge as they will be removed first. When pinning has been completed, remove the tape, roll carefully, take the bundle to a more comfortable location, and fasten the safety pins. (Members of the family can be recruited for this process.)

If possible, avoid placing pins on quilting lines, if you know their positions ahead of time. Pins are of course removed as necessary during the quilting process. Order an adequate supply of pins. It takes nearly 1,000 to pin baste a large quilt. If safety pins are not available, use straight pins followed by thread basting. However, this greatly prolongs the whole process.

THREAD

My thread choice is 100% cotton for machine quilting, either the quilting thread or "silk finish." Both work very well. It is available in well over 200 colors. Do not use regular silicone-treated thread on the machine.

While considering the design, also keep in mind the thread color. Remember the machine stitching line looks harsh. To diminish this, lower the contrast and use matching thread as much as possible. Light color thread on dark fabric is far less obtrusive than dark thread on light fabrics. Match the bobbin thread to the backing. Change both top and bottom thread colors as frequently as necessary.

THE DESIGN

No matter how competent your fine quilting, if the design does not fill the space adequately, it will not enhance the overall piece. This is one of the most important considerations to be faced, and is frequently the most difficult. I included optional quilting designs for all projects, but first, try to create your own.

The traditional method of quilting ¼" away from each seam line is not practical by machine nor would it add any texture or dimension. Not only would it take forever to weave in all the beginnings and endings, but would be extremely boring as well.

If the project is important, try to create an exciting special design unique to the project itself. Remember the old adage..."Whatever is worth doing at all, is worth doing well" (Philip Dormer Stanhope, Earl of Chesterfield, 1746). You do not want your quilt to look like a mattress pad or pre-quilted fabric.

The quilting design should look as if it were designed specifically for the quilt, not simply a purchased stencil you happened to like. A good design should have some relationship to the patchwork design itself. If it distracts and detracts from the beauty of the top, it is not appropriate.

Frequently, you may have to decide whether or not the border is a separate entity and needs to be quilted as a frame apart from the central portion. Or, can you include it in the overall design extending out to the edge of the piece? If you enjoy puzzles and mazes, chances are pretty good you will enjoy this process. Sometimes the solution comes quickly, but it sometimes can take weeks before you are satisfied. The challenge is to begin at one location and arrive at another without stopping yet adding line, dimension, and texture, all at the same time.

Plan a design that has as few inside beginnings and endings as possible. Those at the very outside edge, a logical place to start, will eventually be covered by the binding and will not require weaving or hiding in the ditch. If a line of stitching must begin in the open, leave 4" to 5" lengths of thread to be woven in by hand.

Whatever your chosen design, it should fill the spaces consistently without an over abundance in one area and large unquilted spaces in another. Robbie Fanning, in her book *The Complete Book of Machine Quilting*, suggests the "fist test." If you place your fist on the quilt and no line of stitching touches it, then additional quilting is needed.

Look at the negative space (the background), a nonprominent part of the design. That area most likely will be quilted down thereby "puffing up" or emphasizing the major area. Remember, more quilting is flatter – less is puffy.

Stitching in the ditch, the area immediately adjacent to a seam line away from the pressed direction, is fast and functional, requires little brain work, but usually fails to add creativity, line, or dimension. However, in conjunction with other design elements, it is very appropriate. Make sure any ditch stitching remains in the ditch.

Stitching tight little circles and leaves is extremely difficult when using the walking foot, especially on a large quilt. Barbara Johannah, in her book *Continuous Curve Quilting*, proposes using arcs from one intersection to another. Another design source is *Continuous Line Quilting Designs Especially for Machine*

Quilting by Pat Cody. These designs and purchased stencils are all viable alternatives to drafting your own design but are seldom the exact size that you need. But, a little work with graph paper, pencil, and a good eraser, and you can draft designs to fit the necessary space.

If you are quilting a special and important piece, take the time to prepare a scale drawing of the entire quilt, shading or coloring in the entire design. By placing tracing paper over this drawing, you can try many designs, and then discard them before choosing the perfect one. Make your own stencils as necessary, or use tools such as protractors or angles. You derive a great sense of satisfaction and accomplishment if your design is original.

MARKING

A wide variety of fabric markers is available. I most frequently use the original Chakoner® for temporary marking, and General's Multi-Pastel chalk®, light blue pencil #12 for slightly longer lasting marking. Avoid any yellow markers. Some fabrics and threads simply will not release the color. Sharpen pencils frequently.

If you plan to wash your quilt, spray the top with sizing or starch prior to marking and the markings will wash off easily. I prefer not to starch the fabrics before they go into the quilt for fear the scrap basket will attract bugs.

THE PROCEDURE

When you are finally ready to quilt, clear off plenty of space, remove any make-up if the quilt is large, and get comfortable. Rest your elbows, if possible, and take frequent breaks. Marathon machine quilting sessions will result in aching arms and shoulders, and shin splints are a distinct possibility.

Machine stitch the entire perimeter first, slightly less than ¼" from the raw edge. Remove the straight pins as you go. Now is a good time to check the stitch length. I prefer nine stitches to the inch, but the length used is optional of course.

Also check stitch tension at this point. If using two contrasting threads (light on top and dark in the bobbin for example), it is nearly impossible to avoid a small pin-prick of color on one side. It is better to have this occur on the back. To accomplish this, lower the top tension slightly. Another solution is to always match the thread color of both top and bottom threads. If you have a problem with puckering, try a single stitch throat plate.

Because you cannot get your fingers underneath, it does not matter where you begin stitching. Therefore, I nearly always begin with the border so as many pins as possible can be removed before the harsh handling begins. Stitch all straight lines first to anchor the piece sufficiently prior to lifting and turning.

Start with a full bobbin and check it occasionally, especially before beginning a long track or row. Running out of thread in the middle is a nuisance and means additional ends to weave in or hide.

To secure stitches at the beginning of a track, use a very short stitch length for about ¼" just enough to move forward. Repeat this at the end. If the new quilting line begins at a location other than the edge, make sure it is neatly hidden in the ditch, or leave 4" to 5" threads to be woven in by hand later. If weaving is necessary, I recommend doing it as soon as the track has been completed. Do not save it for later. Each track means four threads – two on top and two on bottom.

A large flat area is essential. Move the entire quilt bundle as a single package. The area being quilted should be completely relaxed, not stretched or distorted in any way. Avoid the temptation to pull or put a drag on the quilt. Allow the walking foot and the feed dogs to work together. A very slight speed bump pushed directly in front of the presser foot with your finger works well to help prevent puckers, especially if there is excess fullness in an area.

When changing direction, always stop with the needle down. A seam allowance is a natural stopping place. Any discrepancy in the stitch length will be less noticeable. You will need to adjust the entire bundle many times.

QUICK SUMMARY
1. Good equipment
2. Flat batting
3. Busy backing fabric
4. Proper sandwich preparation
5. Thread color
6. Good design
7. Marking
8. Quilting

Chapter Seven — Binding

What a relief to see a well-applied binding. It can "make" a quilt. An integral part of the piece, it should not be an afterthought. It should not be slapped on just to get finished. There are many ways to finish an edge. The method in this chapter is what works best for me. I encourage you to explore other methods until you find one that works best for you.

The primary function of a binding is to enclose and protect the raw edges. It should be consistent in width and firmly filled with batting without distortion or puckering. Use fabric of the same fiber content and quality as the quilt itself. Avoid commercially packaged binding. It has not been pre-shrunk and will not coordinate as well nor be as durable as your own prepared binding. The color is your choice. It may match the border fabric or may be an additional personal design statement. Neither the color nor the width should be distracting. I personally prefer a width of just a bit more than 1/4". Regularly patterned fabric, pin dots for example, should be avoided. A strange distracting, twisting appearance results. Choose the binding fabric carefully.

The quilt judges frequently agree to disagree on various quiltmaking techniques, among them: the width of the binding itself, whether or not the fabric is cut with the straight of grain or cross grain, whether or not the front width is identical to the back width, and whether or not the folds of the mitered corner are stitched closed. There are no rules! However, they do agree that corners should be consistent, square (if applicable), and flat without cupping or dog-eared (splayed).

MEASURING

Using a walking foot, machine stitch approximately 3/16" from the raw edges around the entire perimeter of the quilt. Using a large 1/8" thick Plexiglas® ruler and a rotary cutter on a cutting mat, square the corners and clean finish the raw edges. Measure the perimeter and set aside.

The binding strips will have to be joined on all but the smallest quilts. I prefer to use the cross grain of the fabric

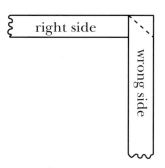

Figure 7-1.

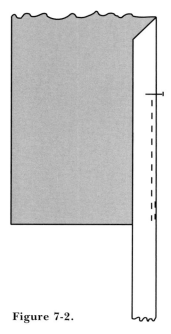

Figure 7-2.

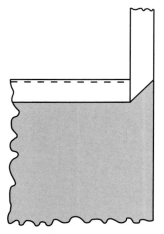

Figure 7-3.

because it gives just a bit, but I will use the straight of grain if the quantity or the design of the fabric dictates it. Bias binding is necessary only when edges or corners are curved.

Cut 2¼" wide strips of fabric to measure 10 inches longer than the perimeter of the quilt. Splice these strips together as shown in Figure 7-1. It is done in this manner to distribute the bulk of the seam allowance over a wider area so it is not all in one spot. Trim seams to ¼" and press open.

At one end, cut a 45° angle in the same direction as the mitered joining seam. Press long raw edges together, right side out. The folded binding will measure 1⅛" by the perimeter measurement plus a few inches, depending on the number of joins.

APPLYING THE BINDING

Before actually stitching, it is a good idea to "walk" the binding around the perimeter including the folding, to make sure that none of the joining seams coincide with the corner miters.

Matching all raw edges of the quilt sandwich and both edges of the folded binding (angled end), pin together about 15" away from any corner. With the walking foot, begin stitching about 6" away from the corner, taking a ¼" seam allowance, and using 10 to 12 stitches to the inch. (The remainder of the binding will be stitched later.)

Approach the corner slowly. Stop stitching when the seam appears to be ¼" away from the raw edge. With the needle down, pivot the entire quilt to check that the next edge will be lined up exactly with the edge of the presser foot. If not, pivot back to the original position and take an additional stitch or two as necessary. When perfect, pivot to original position and backstitch five or six stitches into the seam allowance (Figure 7-2). Clip threads only and remove the work from the machine. **Do not cut binding.**

Place work on a flat surface. Fold binding up as shown in Figure 7-3, aligning it with the next edge. Next, fold the binding straight down (Figure 7-4) matching the raw edges and having the folded binding lined up squarely with the top edge. Backstitch about ¼" toward the top edge and continue stitching forward toward the next corner. Repeat for all corners. Accuracy is very important.

As you approach the original starting point, leave an additional 6" to 8" length of binding unstitched. Remove work from the machine and gently smooth and pin the unstitched binding in place. Fold the binding end up at a 90° angle to exactly match the angled beginning piece (Figure 7-5). Finger crease the binding. **Unfold** binding to its original 2¼" width, and add ½" seam allowance to finger-creased fold. Cut binding on the newly added diagonal line.

Pin single thicknesses of the binding (beginning end and ending end) right sides together, using ¼" seam allowance as shown in Figure 7-6. Match folds ¼" away from the raw edge. Stitch seam and press open. Re-fold and press. Pin, and stitch the remaining section to the quilt.

FINISHING

Smooth the binding to the back, over the edge of the batting, and blindstitch securely using thread to match the binding and your best hand appliqué stitch. Pin only a small area at a time; 3 or 4 pins is sufficient.

The corners will miter on both sides, the front automatically. Looking at the back side, corner upward, fold right side over first, then the left side, making sure the folds meet at the inner angle. Pin in place.

When stitching the corners, blindstitch the folded edge of the miter almost to the point. Insert the needle through all thicknesses. Close the front miter, then return to the back and resume stitching the next side. Make sure the securing stitches do not go through to the right side of the quilt.

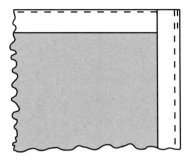

Figure 7-4.

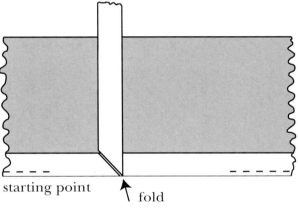

starting point fold

Figure 7-5.

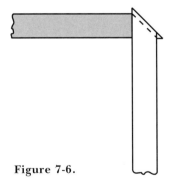

Figure 7-6.

Chapter Eight — Finishing

A QUILT IN EVERY ROOM!

Whether or not you plan to enter your quilt into competition, you may want to make a sleeve to display it. Quilts are works of art, and walls look wonderful covered with quilts! A sleeve or tube will protect the quilt itself from contact with wood or metal holders.

Match the sleeve to the backing fabric if possible to minimize the distraction particularly if your quilt is being sent to competition. Measure the width of the quilt from edge to edge including the binding. Cut the sleeve fabric to this measurement by 9" deep, piecing if necessary. Press all piecing seams open. Narrowly hem both short edges. Stitch long edges wrong sides together. Press the seam open centering the seam on one side of the sleeve/tube. With this seam placed face down on the quilt, it will not be visible.

Matching the centers of the quilt and the sleeve, pin the sleeve in place just inside the binding. Blindstitch, leaving the top layer of the sleeve unstitched at the ends. The thread color should match the sleeve.

SIGNING

The quilt is not quite done yet. It needs to be signed. You may know who made it and when, but sometime in the future someone else will be curious. Hopefully, your family members will be interested.

INFORMATION

The absolute minimum information should include your name, including your full middle or maiden name, and the date. Other helpful information is the title, a location, the name of the recipient, if applicable, and any particular reason the quilt was made.

Additional information may include the dates started and completed, the pattern source or inspiration, size, fabrics and batting used, shows entered, awards received, and current owner.

If the information you wish to include is lengthy, make a small pocket and attach it to the back of the quilt and insert a typed page. A photograph is frequently included.

TECHNIQUE

If you are good at embroidery, by all means use this skill on the front or on the back of the quilt. Other methods include cross stitching, writing with permanent pens, typing on fabric (press to freezer paper or spray starch the fabric).

My husband has printed wonderful signature labels for me on his computer/printer, which I then trace on the fabric with a permanent pen.

FINAL THOUGHTS

Every quilt-related book I pick up inspires me or plants an idea, but two other books totally unrelated to quiltmaking have been great inspirations to me, mainly to get me going, to change my thinking, and to force me to ask what if..., and why not. They are *A Kick in the Seat of the Pants* and *A Whack on the Side of the Head* by Roger von Oech.

I hope this book will trigger your imagination also.

Beyer, Jinny. *Patchwork Patterns*. McLean, Virginia: EPM Publications, 1979.

_____. *The Quilter's Album of Blocks and Borders*. McLean, Virginia: EPM Publications, 1980.

_____. *The Scraplook: Designs, Fabrics, Colors and Piecing Techniques for Creating Multi-Fabric Quilts*. McLean, Virginia: EPM Publications, 1985.

Brackman, Barbara. *Encyclopedia of Pieced Quilt Patterns*. Paducah, Kentucky: American Quilter's Society, 1993.

Caron, Barbara. *Tessellations and Variations: Design Ideas for One and Two-Patch Quilts*. Morgantown, West Virginia, 1986.

_____. *Tessellations and Variations: Design Ideas for One and Two-Patch Quilts, Revised Edition, New Chapters on History and Design*. St. Paul, Minnesota, 1989.

Cody, Pat. *Continuous Line Quilting Designs Especially for Machine Quilting*. Radnor, Pennsylvania: Chilton Book Company, 1984.

Dietrich, Mimi. *Happy Endings – Finishing the Edges of Your Quilt*. Bothell, Washington: That Patchwork Place, 1987.

Fanning, Robbie. *The Creative Machine Newsletter*. Menlo Park, California: Open Chain Publishing, Inc.

Fanning, Robbie and Tony Fanning. *The Complete Book of Machine Quilting*. Radnor, Pennsylvania: Chilton Book Company, 1980.

Hall, Carrie A. and Rose G. Kretsinger. *The Romance of the Patchwork Quilt in America*. Caldwell, Idaho: The Caxton Printers, Ltd., 1935.

Hargrave, Harriet. *Heirloom Machine Quilting*. Westminster, California: Burdett Publications, 1987.

Holstein, Jonathan. *The Pieced Quilt: An American Design Tradition*. Boston: New York Graphic Society, 1973.

Johannah, Barbara. *Continuous Curve Quilting – Machine Quilting the Pieced Quilt*. Menlo Park, California: Pride of the Forest, 1980.

Marston, Gwen and Joe Cunningham. *Sets & Borders*. Paducah, Kentucky: American Quilter's Society, 1987.

McClun, Diana and Laura Nownes. *Quilts! Quilts!! Quilts!!! The Complete Guide to Quiltmaking*. San Francisco, California: The Quilt Digest Press, 1988.

Morris, Patricia J. *The Ins & Outs: Perfecting the Quilting Stitch*. Paducah, Kentucky: American Quilter's Society, 1990.

Penders, Mary Coyne. *Color and Cloth*. San Francisco, California: The Quilt Digest Press, 1989.

Rehmel, Judy. *Key to 1000 Quilt Patterns*. Richmond, Indiana: 1978.

_____. *Key to a Second 1000 Quilt Patterns*, 1979.

_____. *Key to a Third 1000 Quilt Patterns*, 1980.

Shirer, Marie. *Quilt Settings*. Wheatridge, Colorado: Moon Over the Mountain Publishing Company, 1989.

_____. *The Quilters' How-To-Dictionary*. Wheatridge, Colorado: Leman Publications, 1991.

Smith, Lois. *Fun & Fancy Machine Quiltmaking*. Paducah, Kentucky: American Quilter's Society, 1989.

von Oech, Roger. *A Kick in the Seat of the Pants*. New York, New York: Harper and Row Publishers, Inc., 1986.

_____. *A Whack on the Side of the Head* (rev.). New York, New York: Warner Books, Inc., 1990.

Wagner, Debra. *Teach Yourself Machine Piecing & Quilting*. Radnor, Pennsylvania: Chilton Book Company, 1992.

Williamson, Darra Duffy. *Sensational Scrap Quilts*. Paducah, Kentucky: American Quilter's Society, 1993.

Resource List

Clotilde Inc.
2 Sew Smart Way B 8031
Stevens Point, WI 54481-8031
(catalog: $2.00)

Crazy Ladies and Friends
1606 Santa Monica Blvd.
Santa Monica, CA 90404
mail order: (310)207-6529
Brass pins and other supplies

G Street Fabrics Mail Order Service
12240 Wilkins Ave.
Rockville, MD 20852
(301)231-8960

Keepsake Quilting
Rt. 25B
PO Box 1618
Centre Harbor, NH 03226-1618
(catalog: $1.00)

Nancy's Notions
PO Box 683
Beaver Dam, WI 53916-9976
(800)765-0690

Quilts and Other Comforts
1 Quilters Lane
PO Box 4100
Golden, CO 80402-4100

Redex
PO Box 939
Salem, OH 44460
Udder Cream, hand protection

The Stencil Company
PO Box 1218
Williamsville, NY 14221-1218
(716)656-9430
continuous line stencils, marking pencils, and other supplies

TreadleArt
25834-1 Narbonne Ave.
Lomita, CA 90717
(213)534-5122
orders: (800)327-4222
Sewing and Quilting Supply Catalog: $3.00, all kinds of machine supplies, especially walking feet

Vintage Tools and Textiles
PO Box 265
Merion, PA 19066
antique tools, tops, quilts, and other collectibles

∾ American Quilter's Society ∾
dedicated to publishing books for today's quilters